Manipulating Needs
Capitalism and Culture

Manipulating Needs
Capitalism and Culture

CONRAD LODZIAK

Pluto Press
LONDON • BOULDER, COLORADO

First published 1995 by Pluto Press
345 Archway Road, London N6 5AA
and 5500 Central Avenue
Boulder, Colorado 80301, USA

British Library Cataloguing in Publication Data
A catalogue record for this book is available from
the British Library

ISBN 0 7453 0853 8 hbk

Library of Congress Cataloging in Publication Data
Lodziak, Conrad.
    Manipulating needs: capitalism and culture / Conrad
    Lodziak.
        p.   cm.
    Includes bibliographical references and index.
    ISBN 0–7453–0853–8
    1. Postmodernism—Philosophy. 2. Capitalism. 3. Culture.
    4. Ideology. 5. Socialism. I. Title.
    HM73.L62 1995
    306.3'42—dc20   94–43646
                                                    CIP

Designed, typeset and produced for Pluto Press by
Chase Production Services, Chipping Norton, OX7 5QR
Printed in Finland by WSOY

Contents

Preface

For much of this century, up to the early 1980s, a central concern of social theory was that of explaining how the advanced capitalist societies managed to remain stable in spite of the existence of fundamental social inequalities. The latter, it was widely assumed, could fuel discontent, destabilising forms of protest, and potentially unleash powerful forces of social change. The most popular explanation for why this has not happened was centred on the view that the vast majority of people had come to accept their subordination to the capitalist class by virtue of ideological manipulation. This explanation, which became known as the 'dominant ideology thesis', was roundly criticised throughout the 1970s and early 1980s. But before the criticisms gelled into a comprehensive, alternative explanation of how capitalist societies reproduce themselves, social theory became embroiled in debate – the modernity/postmodernity debate – about the scale and pace of recent social changes. With a few exceptions there has been little attempt to connect this debate with issues surrounding the reproduction of capitalist societies. In many respects the problem of the reproduction of capitalist societies is no longer an issue in social theory. My initial task is to restore this problem as a central issue. My reasons are political rather than academic.

The most significant changes charted in the modernity/postmodernity debate – the globalisation of capitalism, the declining power of the nation-state, the proliferation of advanced technologies, the technologicalisation of work, the growth of consumerism, the growth of urbanism, the erosion of communities, the fragmentation of the working class, the decline of politics, and so forth – have their source in the growth of capitalism, and contribute to the reproduction of the capitalist system. The main beneficiaries of these changes are the capitalist class and their favoured subordinates. The main victims are the hundreds of millions of people living undernourished, slow deaths in the Third World. On top of this, ecological imbalance, a major consequence of the growth of capitalism, affects everyone. And there are clear signs that the changes generated by capitalism are adversely affecting an increasing proportion of people living in the advanced capitalist societies. The reproduction of capitalism *is* a problem.

Explaining the reproduction of the capitalist system is important in so far as it can provide guidance on how we can best disrupt the system to abolish its most damaging effects. In other words explanations of the reproduction of capitalism inform theories and strategies of emancipatory social change. The dominant ideology thesis, for example, has been influential (and still is) in making 'ideological struggle' the central focus of left-wing politics. The thinking here is that disrupting the reproduction of the capitalist system is dependent on people being won over to accepting oppositional ideas. I devote the second chapter to a discussion of the dominant ideology thesis and its critique. I argue that both the dominant ideology thesis, and some critiques of it, have exaggerated the power of ideology, and underplayed the material power of economic and state practices, in the reproduction of capitalist societies. There are critiques of the dominant ideology thesis that quite rightly reject the view that the political quiescence of the subordinate majority is due to the manipulative effects of the dominant ideology. But in arguing that the subordinate adopt a wide range of ideologies, and that this prevents widespread support for oppositional viewpoints, these critiques remain 'ideology-centred' in their approach to action. Ideology-centred explanations of the reproduction of the capitalist system underpin ideology-centred politics.

At the heart of ideology-centred thinking is the assumption that our actions are governed by our beliefs. Against this view, I argue in the third chapter that actions are better explained in terms of the resources available to the individual, and that for the vast majority actions are needs rather than ideologically motivated. My central thesis is that the reproduction of the capitalist system is most adequately understood in terms of the manipulation of needs.

Needless to say the manipulation of needs thesis provides a radically different account of contemporary culture from the ideology-centred literature on postmodernity. The conservatism of this literature, particularly in its treatments of consumerism and identity, does not make happy reading for the Left. By contrast, the manipulation of needs thesis makes it clear that consumerism, and other contemporary cultural trends, are not the obstacles to emancipatory social change that we have been led to believe.

It is becoming increasingly evident that the capitalist system is pursuing a direction which distances it from what people most need. This, I believe, signals an opportunity to loosen our dependence on the capitalist system, and to create for ourselves the conditions in which our need for a meaningful and satisfying life can be served. It is to this end that this volume is devoted.

ACKNOWLEDGEMENTS

Thanks are due to the *Nottingham Critical Social Theory and Politics Group* – Finn Bowring, Simon Cross, Luke Goode, Ted Hankin, Steve Harper, Josephine Logan, Neil Maycroft, Gabriel Mythen, Paul Ransome, Jim Shorthose, Jeremy Tatman and Steve Taylor.

Thanks are also due to Anne Beech of Pluto Press for her constructive criticisms of the first draft of this book.

1 Introduction: Changing Times and the Left

We hear little these days of the traditional Left project of the class struggle over the ownership and control of the means of production. The class struggle was to culminate in the social control of the economy, enabling production to be motored by the needs of people rather than by the need for profit. The majority, the working class, it was believed, would come to see that the only way of protecting themselves against poverty and misery, and to enjoy the fruits of their own labour, was to break their dependence on the controlling minority, the capitalist class.

That the revolution predicted by Marx has not materialised in the advanced capitalist societies is for the Right proof enough of the triumph of capitalism, that the class struggle is unnecessary and that socialism is misconceived. Those on the Left who identify themselves with class politics are referred to as 'yesterday's men', caught up in a 'politics of envy'. The implication of this characterisation is that they have not moved with the times. If they had they would see that class politics is irrelevant, so the argument goes. Socialism, it is claimed, is neither needed nor viable. The demise of the Soviet Union is not only further proof that socialism does not work but also proof that people don't want it. What people do want is freedom. In short the Right assert that people want the kind of freedom that is available in the advanced capitalist societies.

Needless to say the venom of the ideological onslaught against class politics and socialism suggests that the political representatives of capitalism are not entirely convinced of their own propaganda. To attack the need for class politics and socialism is itself part of class politics. If class politics still exist for the Right things are not so clear for the Left. While the Left have always been divided on issues such as how to win the struggle for socialism, what kind of socialism they should aim to develop, and whether or not they should become involved in struggles for short-term gains, they were nevertheless united in their class sympathies. Improving the conditions of the working class, whether in the workplace or in the wider social environment, was a unifying theme for the Left. This remained the case at least until the early 1960s. Since then class politics has gradually been moved from the centre of left-wing politics. Today there is no centre and there is no unifying theme around which the discontents can be mobilised. Later in this volume I shall be making a case for a potential unifying theme for the Left. For the moment it will be useful to consider some of the reasons why class no longer holds centre stage in Left politics.

The Decline of Working Class Politics

While in theory the labour movement has been committed to the struggle for the ownership and control of the means of production, this has not been the case in practice.[1] The class struggle, for the most part, has centred on wage demands. Additionally energies have been directed at the shortening of the working day, better work conditions, the protection of jobs and the provision, development and, recently, defence of public services. The dominant focus on wage demands is readily accommodated within the capitalist class–working class relation, and does not threaten the control of employers over employees. Furthermore, it fuels competition among workers which undermines the class solidarity necessary for successful class struggle; it steers workers toward privatised consumption – another obstacle to class solidarity – and it provides employers with a handy excuse for job cuts. That employers are more than prepared to do this has, in recent years, taken the militancy out of industrial disputes and spawned a reluctance to strike.

There is a sense then in which a class politics that is

P

largely confined to wage demands undermines itself. This is where we are at today. The feeling that this strategy has had its day permeates the Left. Not that this feeling has emerged as a consequence of the realisation of the inherent limitations of a wage demand strategy, rather there is the growing recognition that we are living in rapidly changing times and that the conditions that brought the labour movement into being no longer exist. Since the early days of the labour movement there has developed an intermediary class, the middle class, largely peopled by the upwardly mobile working class. The middle class, whether they be small business proprietors or professionals of some description, are hardly impoverished. Among the wage earning working class a majority enjoy lifestyles that suggest a degree of affluence rather than deprivation. In these circumstances the language of class exploitation has a rather hollow ring to it.

The changing class situation has posed difficulties for the identity of left-leaning social democratic political parties. Are they to develop policies of welfare and public service to address the needs of the underclass? Or, are they to appeal to the affluent majority, maybe through 'consumer politics'?[2] Even though the poor make up approximately one-quarter of the populations of the advanced capitalist societies, a large percentage do not vote in electoral contests. The logic of electoral competition suggests that social democratic parties should seek support from the affluent, perhaps within a framework of humane capitalism. This does seem to be the favoured direction. Within this development the demise of class politics is also the demise of socialism. Nowhere in the advanced capitalist societies is there a major political party seeking to dismantle capitalism.[3]

The decline of class politics has been facilitated by the emergence of issues that cannot adequately be depicted solely in class terms. Issues concerning male domination, racism, new forms of imperialism, environmental destruction, nuclear disarmament, militarism and civil liberties have all quite rightly found their way on to the modern Left's agenda. In the process the traditional Left has taken a battering. It has been

criticised for harbouring elements of sexism and racism,
and for espousing policies that are ecologically insensitive. There have been, and are, attempts to modernise
the Left by incorporating the concerns of the new
social movements, particularly those of the women's
movement and the Greens, within a broad socialist
programme.[4] While such attempts would seem to be
necessary if the Left is to reconstruct itself as an
effective force for progressive change, they have proved
difficult to sustain. Feminism, for example, is heavily
fragmented, and the Greens do not speak with one
voice.[5] While some feminists are clearly committed to a
socialist feminism, others have different concerns and
priorities. Similarly some Greens see industrial capitalism as the primary source of ecological imbalance, and
are thus open to alliances with socialists, but others
adopt different approaches and are openly hostile to
socialism.

We thus have not only divisions among the Left
but divisions among those like feminists and Greens
who do not identify themselves with the Left but are
opposed to the social system in some way. A fragmented opposition is an ineffective one, unable to
exert sustained pressure for the kinds of changes
sought by the Left and other progressive elements.
Pressure for change, whether directed at the institutions of capitalism or the capitalist state, or at social
democratic parties that might champion progressive
causes, derives in large part from the degree of public
support that can be mobilised. Such support cannot
begin to express itself in the absence of some agency
that is clearly identifiable as capable of carrying public demands. There is no such agency. The fragmentation of the opposition to the social system must be
overcome in the process of creating an effective
agency. Even then it is not clear that the public
would see in such an agency the ideal focus for their
demands. Indeed, if we are to go along with some of
those who depict these changing times as 'postmodern' we would have to question whether or not a
left-wing politics is needed, let alone likely.

Postmodernity and the Left

Throughout the past decade the dominant debate in social and cultural studies, the 'modernity/postmodernity' debate, has among other things highlighted the gathering scale, pace and intensity of economic, political and cultural changes, especially during the past 30 years or so, both globally and locally.

Of all the changes noted that concerning the globalisation of economic institutions and practices is crucial. The capitalist world system is dominated by massive multinational companies and banks. One major consequence of this is that a society's economic activity is increasingly controlled by forces external to it. At the same time this decreases the capacity of governments to govern. This is particularly important for social democratic governments that might want to embark on programmes of wealth redistribution, or improved public and welfare services. Such programmes must be funded by some form of taxation on wealth, and this is obviously unattractive to major companies, who, as Raymond Williams expressed it, are capable of moving their 'millions under various flags of convenience'.[6] In other words multinational companies are well-practised in disinvestment in unfavourable conditions and reinvestment in conditions more conducive to larger profits. In this context leftish programmes are automatically compromised. Policies involving increased public expenditure, no matter how popular, no longer seem possible. In truth they are not possible *within* capitalism. Needless to say those who still adhere to the possibility of a socialist future must contend with a powerful *international* capitalist class. The dismantling of capitalism, given its global dimensions, is a daunting task.

All societies are potentially vulnerable to multinational companies' policies. In the Third World this vulnerability is permanent. Third World societies have to continually convince multinational companies and banks that they provide ideal conditions for profit making. This is achieved primarily by governments developing the 'repressive state apparatus', that is, the forces of law and order, so that they are capable of repressing potential threats to production. There is an acknowledgement that capitalism can produce discontent that is socially destabilising, and thus undermining of itself. The strong state, a necessary evil in Third World societies, has become a growing feature of the advanced capitalist societies. Over the past decade or so in Britain, for example, we have witnessed an erosion of civil liberties, involving among other things, legislation restricting the conduct of industrial disputes in ways that illegalise traditional forms of workers' democracy.[7] In addition there has been an increase in the numbers of police, and a greater preparedness among police to use violence and militaristic strategies and techniques when they see fit.

Largely as a consequence of the investment policies of multinational companies there have been shifts in the location of the sites of production. Many of the advanced capitalist societies have experienced a decline in the heavy manufacturing industries and mining, the traditional strongholds of the labour movement. This has led, many argue, to the fragmentation of the working class. On the one hand workers have been dispersed into smaller work units, and on the other, and connected to this dispersal, traditional working class communities have virtually disappeared. These communities were an important resource in more ways than one, not least for sustaining class struggles.

The development of ever newer technologies and their use in production has had a further fragmenting effect on the working class. As labour becomes increasingly automated, that is, as more and more work functions are given over to the machine, a process heightened under the advent of electronic technology, less labour is required to produce the same volume of goods. Within capitalism reduced labour requirements translates into unemployment. Governments pretend to be concerned about unemployment. In fact unemployment, in so far as it involves a reserve army of labour,

is useful to the capitalist class in depressing wages and
reducing the bargaining power of workers. It serves as
a permanent reminder to would-be strikers that there
are others willing to take their place.

The technologicalisation of work processes has not
only reduced the need for labour but it has also transformed the workforce into a highly skilled elite com-
manding high wages and civilised work conditions, and a
mass of workers performing deskilled functions for lower
pay in relatively poor conditions. Many deskilled jobs are
temporary and/or, part-time negatively promoting self-
employment and a growing reliance on the underground
economy. The latter has become a permanent feature of
regions with high levels of unemployment.[8]

Today then, we have a picture of a highly fragmented workforce with seemingly little in common.
This makes unified class action very difficult. Trade
unions continue to fight for and defend the interests of
their members, but union action does not have the
impact it once did when the bulk of the workforce were
employed in heavy industries and manufacturing.
Unions today are smaller. An increasing proportion of
labour, particularly in the service sector, is non-union-
ised. There appears to be little enthusiasm among those
in deskilled work to engage in labour struggles. This is
understandable in the context of high unemployment
and welfare provision that is increasingly inadequate in
meeting survival needs.

The insecurity that attends temporary, deskilled
work has its parallels in the professions. The threat of
redundancy in one form or another has undermined
career structures and the confidence of the professions.
More than this, self-management, a defining characteristic of a profession, has gradually given way to forms
of management surveillance more typical of the supervi-
sion of deskilled work. Needless to say such surveillance erodes morale and autonomy, encouraging instrumental attitudes toward work as opportunities for
meaning dwindle.

The changes that I have noted with respect to the
nature and form of work are by no means uniform.

There is, however, a measure of agreement among those addressing the identifiable characteristics of post-modernity that these changes are sufficiently underway to warrant a depiction of the postmodern social order in which production and work are no longer of central importance. Consumption rather than production, it is often argued, has become the organising principle both of society and individual life. Thus Zygmunt Bauman proposes that:

> in present-day society, consumer conduct (consumer freedom geared to the consumer market) moves steadily into the position of, simultaneously, the cognitive and moral focus of life, the integrative bond of the society, and the focus of systemic management. In other words, it moves into the selfsame position which in the past – during the 'modern' phase of capitalist society – was occupied by work in the form of wage labour. This means that in our time individuals are engaged (morally by society, functionally by the social system) first and foremost as consumers rather than as producers.[9]

For those who believe this to be fundamentally true, left-wing politics, traditionally oriented to production and producers, needs to be radically reformulated in order to be socially relevant and in touch with individuals. As Bauman goes on to point out, 'for the consumer, reality is not the enemy of pleasure'.[10]

Obviously if people want what the social system is already providing there is no need to change the system. And if the controllers of the system, the capitalist class, benefit from people wanting what the system provides then it is clear that 'the future of capitalism looks more secure than ever'.[11] One response from the 'Left' is basically 'if you can't beat them, join them'. In arguing for a politics of consumption, Frank Mort asks the left to connect with the ideologies of affluence and individualism which, he feels, should be taken seriously. Consumption, he claims, is important, 'precisely because it touches people where they *feel* active and powerful'.[12] The politics of consumption, for Mort, would attempt to increase the choices available to the consumer, and would attempt to achieve some form of socially responsible balance between collective and individual consumption. Hardly radical stuff.

There is no doubt that the attractions of consumerism must be addressed by the Left. If these attractions are as strong as some writers suggest then the Left are in trouble. Consumption is centrally involved in the reproduction of capitalism.

One of the reasons why consumption is viewed as attractive is because it is widely regarded as being the main means through which we construct our identities in postmodern times. Thus Robert Bocock writes that 'consumption has become essential to many men's sense of who they are. It has become as significant as work roles, if not more so, for younger men especially.'[13] Bocock is already assuming that consumption has long been established as central to identity construction for women. Be that as it may, identity issues do loom large. Matters relevant to self-identity, for example, health, diet, fitness, appearance, fashion, sexuality, psychology, attract increasing media coverage. Each of these issues, and more, figure in a rapidly expanding self-help literature. And, of course, these developments are reflected in a recent upsurge in academic interest and publishing.

All sorts of reasons are on offer to explain the contemporary concern with self-identity. The fragmentation of the working class and the break-up of traditional working class communities, it has been argued, have undermined the traditional identity-building blocks of the working class. No longer able to identify themselves with their work, if they have got any, and uprooted from tightly-knit communities, the working class are searching for new identities. Consistent with earlier arguments, it is claimed that new identities are being forged via the symbolic value of consumer goods and leisure interests. This view is often supplemented by, or even replaced by, an argument that stresses the impact of the ideology of individualism in promoting forms of self-absorption within privatised leisure and consumption. In a similar vein others argue that a characteristic of postmodernity is the proliferation of ideologies or world views as distinct from an earlier period when one or two world views tended to dominate. As a consequence a vast range of ideas or meanings are available for us to make sense of ourselves and our experiences. This context, it is maintained, is conducive to the continuous construction and reconstruction of an endless range of individualities. Such a view is incorporated within a much broader treatment of the current concern with self-identity advanced by Anthony Giddens. Giddens argues that 'nothing is more central to, and distinctive of human life than the reflexive monitoring of behaviour, which is expected by all "competent" members of society of others'.[14] It can be said that the self *is* reflexive, that is, we are aware of what we do and use this awareness as we go about our business in everyday life. But, 'in the context of a post-traditional order, the self becomes a *reflexive project*'.[15] In other words the self is chosen, so to speak. We make and remake ourselves. For Giddens this project materialises itself in our lifestyles. He notes that 'in conditions of high modernity, we all not only follow lifestyles, but in an important sense are forced to do so – we have no choice but to choose'.[16] We have no choice but to choose because we are confronted 'with a complex diversity of choices'.[17]

On the face of it the current concern with self-identity would seem to suggest that the direction of people's lives runs counter to most left-wing projects. In other words there is a tremendous gulf between the concerns of the Left and the concerns that are uppermost in most people. Yet many see in issues centred on self-identity the prospects for a new politics. Until very recently what has become known as the politics of identity was seen as a form of new Left politics. This was so because identity politics gave rise to movements that addressed forms of domination other that class. Part of the struggle against male domination or racism, for example, involved challenging the dominant representations of women and black people since these (mis)representations were materialised in institutional practices that affected life chances. While male and racial domination exist there will always be a need for political opposition, whether in the form of a politics of identity or within some broader emancipatory project.

Concerns with the emancipation of social groups are part and parcel of left-wing politics. More recently, however, emancipatory concerns, which necessarily involve contestation over resources with the powers that be, have been sidelined in identity politics. Issues concerning gendered, sexual and ethnic forms of self-presentation and representation, and self-expression have come to the forefront. This, it is often said, is in keeping with postmodern culture, particularly its emphasis on surface appearance and style. Differences are exaggerated and with it the loss of common purpose central to effective politics. The resulting divisiveness and fragmentation have been widely noted.[18] Identity politics, as currently practised, share little in common with left-wing concerns.

A different kind of identity politics, according to Giddens, is emerging in the form of what he calls 'life politics', which he defines as follows:

> life politics concerns political issues which flow from processes of self-actualisation in post-traditional contexts, where globalising influences intrude deeply into the reflexive project of the self, and conversely where processes of self-realisation influence global strategies.[19]

Giddens offers several examples of life-political issues, including personal decisions about reproduction and contraception, health and diet. He explores the ways in which such concerns raise existential and moral questions and fan out into questions of global concern. Basically he argues that personal decisions can have effects of global importance, and our awareness of this enters into life-planning and the choices that flow from this. We may, for example, given our awareness of the need of the planet to be in ecological balance, change our patterns of consumption.

No doubt something akin to a life politics is emerging but whether this politics makes much difference in the total order of things must be doubted. Often the connections between choices concerning self-identity and global issues are remote and may fuel feelings of powerlessness – the exact opposite of the purpose of politics. Further a focus on the self, whether it be in terms of appearance, diet, sexuality or love-making, may be more aptly representative of privatism than politics. Whether or not postmodern culture is as self-absorbed as Christopher Lasch argues must, for the moment, remain an open question.[20] Privatism, in one form or another, nevertheless does seem to be a growing characteristic of these changing times. As such any politics that are dependent on collective participation must not only contend with the concerns of individuals but must also contend with the widespread feeling that privatistic solutions to experienced problems are more likely to be effective than participation in politics.

The Decline of Political Culture

Rosalind Brunt accurately observes that:

> The way to characterise the present situation of Britain entering the 1990s is in terms of a gaping disparity: a tiny minority of various strands of the British left and progressive movement busy rethinking and reviewing its politics while the vast majority of British people continue to anathematise the very idea of being involved in politics of any sort.[21]

I have already noted how changes over the past 30 years or so have been perceived by many to have created a gulf between the concerns of the Left and those of the general public. These changes and others, François Lyotard has argued, have so undermined the thinking underpinning the traditional Left project that major emancipatory social transformations no longer seem feasible.[22] This view has become influential in intellectual culture and has led to a wide-ranging critique of Marxism and liberalism as sources of theoretical authority. Not only is the validity of Marxist and liberal concepts for social analysis challenged, but they are widely regarded as irrelevant to the experience of today's individuals. Some see in this the principal cause of the gulf between the Left and the general public. The Left, it is maintained, are out of touch with what people think. Furthermore it is suggested that what the Left consider to be a decline in political culture is, in fact, a transition to a diverse one, no longer dominated by organised politics.

I will want to maintain that as long as capitalism exists Marxist theory will be indispensable for social analysis. I will also want to maintain that as long as capitalism exists there will be a need for a Left. The Left, however, won't get very far unless it addresses people's lived experience. One of the important tasks for the Left is to understand why people have become alienated from organised politics. Typically this alienation has been understood as some kind of failing of the individual, perhaps a reflection of 'false consciousness'. I shall deal with this kind of thinking in the next chapter. For the moment I want to take seriously the view that proposes that organised politics themselves have been and still are a major cause of political alienation.

It is not difficult to discern some of the roots of indifference, contempt or even hostility toward organised politics. In a world of rapid change, the official politicians, for all their huff and puff, make very little difference of a positive kind. If anything they are widely perceived as making things worse. One can point to notable exceptions, but these are either marginalised by the party or movement, or swallowed up in its machinery. Generally people have little patience for politicians pontificating about major problems when their solutions seem woefully inadequate. People, too, are plainly aware that party politicians want their votes, and will patronisingly tell them what they think they want to hear.

The main medium of communication of party politics is television. The prospect of communicating with a mass audience is approached not so much as an opportunity to exercise political leadership, but more as an exercise in caution. Messages are delivered in double- or triple-speak. They become bland, cleansed of anything that might offend the voter. All major parties play the same game, and consequently their messages are fundamentally the same. True to the propaganda of liberal democracy that has it that voters are free to vote for the party of their own choosing, the politicians oblige the public by exaggerating trivial party differences. Considerable energy and even more hot air sustain the exaggerated differences. The public, more often than not, quite rightly fail to see what all the fuss is about.

As Claus Offe has argued, the standardisation of political party programmes, which is exacerbated by the parties' use of television, signals a deradicalisation of the major political parties. This has important implications. The lack of clear differences between the parties makes it difficult for them to act as means of collective identification. No longer serving as a means of collective identity, political parties cannot attract, as they once did, committed rank and file members. The hard core of rank and file members that remain find themselves increasingly distanced from the party elite as the latter continue to mould their messages and style to a fictitious 'average' television audience.[23] Party elites have become star performers in a rather boring game.

The logic of party competition requires a centralised party bureaucracy competent in party organisation and financial management. Whatever the party, their elites are increasingly drawn from professionals with the required relevant experience; hence the similarities between parties. Today this professional competence is manifesting itself in the marketing of images to which political programmes and politicians are subordinated.

The loss of the traditional substance of politics, its policies, sense of collective solidarity and passion, and its reconstitution into the form of image, has had a damaging impact on left social democratic parties. For the poor in particular, politics as image signals the loss of a potential resource for the improvement of life-chances. Only years of resignation to little or no opportunity, which prepares the individual for further restrictions, prevents the eruption of anger at the loss of hope once represented by parties of progressive change.

The vast majority, however, in the advanced capitalist societies are not poor. They are able to finance some improvements in their private lives. Obviously very few are able to transform their lifestyles for the reason that income is insufficient to restructure the social conditions in which they are immersed. Nevertheless some progress is possible through private consumption. Although luck does play an unpredictable part, most people make progress. For many it seems that progress comes from their own efforts. To be sure, this progress can be temporarily halted by loss of employment, illness or accident, and for some it is more or less permanently halted.

Those making progress through private consumption want to protect what they have (achieved) and want to get on with their private lives without interference. They react to party politics with indifference because of its seeming irrelevance to what concerns them most, and at times they react with hostility, as when political interference is seen as potentially disruptive of the progress they have made. The privatistic route to improving life is a practical response to the prevailing social conditions. People will put their energies into activities from which they can derive tangible rewards. For most people these activities are in the private sphere. While it is recognised that the satisfactions of the private sphere fall a long way short of some utopian existence, in the absence of any realistic route to the latter the private sphere provides the best bet, at least for the time being, for improving one's life. No realistic utopia is on offer from any of the major political parties. In fact there is very little on offer that would make an appreciable difference to the majority.

All this is not to say that capitalism, by fuelling private consumption, satisfies the vast majority, and thus works. Rather the private sphere offers a minimum amount of satisfaction, just sufficient to encourage people to pursue privatism rather than political change. It would be wrong to see this as an expression of an ideological commitment to individualism or of a motivation based on consumerist greed. Most people are motivated to improve their lives in the practical ways available. With the decline of politics this takes a privatistic rather than collectivist form. People will act collectively when it is in their perceived interests to do so. They will not get involved in political activity where the likely gains are minimal or ambiguous. They quite rightly think that much political activity consumes energies that might be more successfully used in the private realm. Thus Theodor Adorno referred to:

> the by no means unjustified feeling of the masses that political participation within the sphere society grants them ... can alter their actual existence only minimally. Failing to discern the relevance of politics to their own interests, they retreat from all political activity.[24]

The structure and organisation of major political parties, as I have intimated, do not invite participation. Indeed the major parties are organised primarily for electoral competition in which the *support* of voters, rather than their participation is valued. This transforms the relation between party and people into one that is essentially identical to the relation between advertiser and consumer. The hard sell comes at election time. The relation between party and people is, for all intents and purposes, a top-down one. Occasionally pressures from below may have some influence, but by and large the leaders continue in a way that suggests that they think they know what is best. Needless to say this does not encourage the expression of opinion, and in time it discourages the very formation of opinion. This is the trend *within* parties, let alone among the voters. Jürgen Habermas has referred to 'political parties which have migrated from the life-world into the political system'.[25] Yet many experience their participation within a political party in ways that suggest that politics itself have migrated from the political party. Rudolf Bahro thus reached the conclusion that 'at last I have understood that a party is a counterproductive tool, that the given political space is a trap into which life energy disappears, indeed, where it is rededicated to the spiral of death'.[26]

Political parties have indeed become obstacles, both to members and the general public, in the formation, expression and mobilisation of opinion. As such they have become anti-democratic forces, transmitting 'the will of the state to the people, instead of the reverse', as André Gorz has argued.[27] Part of this trend is the growing marginalisation of the system of liberal democracy within society. Of course this system is the very one that has encouraged the depoliticisation of political parties. Nevertheless it is the case that more and more decisions that affect the whole society are made outside of parliament. Gorz has stated it as follows:

> The gulf between public life and social life widens as does that between the general interest and individual interests, and between electoral themes and systemic constraints, bringing about a continual expansion of the spheres of competence of the civil service and the regulatory powers of the state, whilst the parliamentary institutions become a mere shadow theatre.[28]

Yet in spite of the limitations of liberal democracy and the decline of political culture some do seek opportunities to participate in processes of meaningful change. Increasingly social movements are perceived to be more attractive than political parties as vehicles for political participation. Social movements are not encumbered with the bureaucratic machinery of parties. They have more flexible forms of organisation, and more democratic and egalitarian relations among members. They have the decided advantage, too, in being more focused on particular issues.

However, the new social movements tend to reflect little more than protest potentials. Some have been particularly effective in mobilising protest through intensive campaigns and the organisation of demonstrations.[29] There is no doubt that the peace, women's, and ecological movements have influenced public opinion. Agnes Heller and Ferenc Fehér refer to movements as having 'the role of forging political options', whereas parties 'have almost exclusively become economic agencies'.[30] It is rare, however, even for the massive demonstrations to have an impact on the policies of governments or multinational enterprises.

While the very presence of social movements indicates that political culture has not been entirely eroded, their political effectiveness is limited by their inability to sustain 'movement'. The new social movements do not maintain the kind of political presence achieved by the labour movement. The new movements tend to lie dormant for long periods, showing little sign of movement other than internal fragmentation.

It would seem, then, that new social movements are attractive in terms of the kinds of issues they raise but are insufficiently attractive to sustain participation from more than a hard core of committed activists. One of the reasons for this is that new movements tend to remain focused on ideological or moral issues to the relative neglect of social relations among members. They do, after all, mobilise support because of their ideological stance. Yet unless conditions for mutual support and solidarity are established, the focus on the ideological can be extremely divisive. New recruits soon discover that each grouping within a movement has its own particular brand of political correctness and with it a moralism that stifles communication by inhibiting self-expression. It is under these circumstances that loose groupings often develop into fixed, exclusive groups, within which divisive differences are more or less obliterated. Exclusive groups are, by definition, obstacles to wider participation, and their separateness tends to make them politically impotent.

It is hardly surprising that the new social movements have a high turnover of membership. In addition to the focus on ideology, a contributory factor is the interactive and communicative style that tends to predominate. As Herbert Kitschelt has pointed out the style is one that is more palatable to middle class and professional recruits than it is to working class recruits.[31] It is certainly the case that the working class recruits drop in and drop out of participation in the new movements at a faster rate than middle class recruits.

We have seen that neither political parties nor the new social movements are capable of sustaining participation. If the Left is to have a future it will have to question seriously the way in which politics is conducted. Failure to make participation in politics more attractive will merely reinforce common perceptions of 'politicos' as a breed apart, and will continue to widen the gulf between political organisations and the vast majority of people. Somehow the Left must connect with people, and this means first and foremost a deeper exploration of people's motivations.

The Exposure of Identity Needs

Too many on the Left have been too ready to concede that the privatisation of social life and the attractions of consumerism indicate trends that have put emancipatory politics on hold for the foreseeable future, or even maybe forever. What enables this judgement is the view that the new individualism, with its preoccupation with consumerism and self-identity, has taken root as a powerful motivation among the populations of the advanced capitalist societies.

Earlier I noted that issues relevant to self-identity have become prominent in contemporary society. Since self-identity refers to the constellation of meanings an individual attributes to herself or himself, the 'search' for identity is essentially a search for meaning. Recent writing makes much of the expanding opportunities for the construction and reconstruction of identities that exist in postmodern times. But the range of choices confronting the individual, some argue, poses problems. There is much talk of cultural diversity and lifestyle options, and the proliferation of the symbolic value of consumer products. As a consequence the individual cannot escape the problem of picking her or his way through all these choices in constructing an identity. The problem of the search for identity does not necessarily have negative connotations for it reflects an emerging 'ethos of self-growth'.[32]

On closer examination, however, the real problem facing individuals is not so much that of constructing an identity but constructing and maintaining a *meaningful and satisfying* one. Recent mental health statistics reveal that all is not well even among those who are prospering in the centres of affluence. In Britain, for example, the Mental Health Foundation reported in 1990 that six million people were being treated for medically identified mental illness. To these we can add those who are mentally ill but are not identified as such, those who are identified but who are not receiving treatment, and those who seek help from agencies outside of the medical profession.[33] This suggests that a significant proportion of the population do not experience the multitude of choices that are available as *sufficiently meaningful and satisfying*. In other words whatever the attractions of consumerism, and our new found freedoms, they fail to satisfy what the individual *needs* to sustain a meaningful sense of self.

What might these considerations mean for the Left? To put it bluntly we do not have to be held back in our development of an emancipatory project by the assumption that expressions of individuality and consumerism reflect strong motivations among the public at large. Rather it is evident that the advanced capitalist societies are decreasingly able to meet the identity needs of a growing proportion of people. Herein resides a tremendous opportunity for the Left. If the Left is serious about wanting to connect with the people, then what better way than to begin to address identity needs? I shall explore this opportunity in more detail later. For the moment I merely want to state that what I have in mind bears no resemblance to what I referred to earlier as 'the politics of identity'. The politics of identity, as I have noted, is focused on ideological struggles around representations of particular selves, and has led to fragmentation within groups. To address identity needs, by contrast, means to create conditions that enable the experience of security, of a sense of significance, and of autonomy. The development of these conditions is part and parcel of the development of an *oppositional culture*.

The Colonisation of the Lifeworld

Social relations which are supportive of identity needs are in fact conducive to the development of forms of solidarity based on human concern.[34] Such relations, I shall argue, are not to be seen as the focus or content of political action, but as permeating the *conduct* of emancipatory politics. It is the starting place for redemocratising spheres of life, such as child-rearing, education, welfare and recreation for example, that have become increasingly colonised by commercial interests and by the state's bureaucratic tentacles.

In being caught up in analysing our changing times, social theorists and many on the Left have neglected the fact that some enduring features of society remain. The most significant of these are the structures of the capitalist system that enable capitalism to motor social changes while at the same time securing its own stability. All the significant social changes that we are experiencing, and that in total define postmodernity, are not only occurring within capitalism but are beneficial to the capitalist system, and have been generated by it.

Habermas has alerted us to the growing reach of the logic of capitalism, and the administration that supports it, into the very fabric of contemporary experience. The shorthand for this reach is what he calls the 'colonisation of the lifeworld'. This refers to such phenomena as:

The instrumentalisation of professional life; the mobilisation of the workplace; the extension of competition and performance pressures even into elementary school; the monetarisation of services, relations, and life's stages; the consumerist redefinition of personal life spheres; the bureaucratisation and legal regulation of private and informal spheres of action; and above all the political-administrative incorporation of school, family, education, and cultural reproduction in general ...[35]

In a sense the capitalist system – its enterprises, its institutions, and the capitalist state – has taken on a life of its own, cut off from any input and control from ordinary citizens, but increasingly organises their actions. As a consequence traditional forms of life and their social infrastructures have been eroded. This could be potentially liberating, Habermas argues, in the sense that we have been freed 'from encrusted power relations'.[36] Unless we seize the chance to develop social networks and communities that facilitate self-determination (autonomy) and collective self-determination (democracy) we will be subjected to further encroachments from the social system. Habermas suggests that this will lead to:

the impoverishment of expressive and communicative possibilities which, as far as I can see, remain necessary even in complex societies. These are the possibilities that enable individuals to find themselves, to deal with their personal conflicts, and to solve their common problems by means of collective will-formation.[37]

The colonisation of the life-world thesis enables us to appreciate the sources of the contemporary crises of meaning and identity in the advanced capitalist societies. In these societies the capitalist system is granting a majority consumer autonomy. At the same time, and consistent with this, it has been busy in commodifying experiences and human relations, and in formally regulating spheres of life that were once open to informal or democratic control, or left for individuals to sort out for themselves.[38] In other words a majority have been steered toward a trivial and relatively meaningless form of autonomy, and have been denied autonomy in more important and more meaningful matters.

The more autonomy a person is able to exercise the more the self-investment in experience and action, and thus the greater are the possibilities of experiencing meaning. The expansion of autonomy then is not only central to a fulfilling identity, it is also central to improving the quality of one's life. Given the erosion of opportunities for meaningful autonomy it is hardly surprising that identity crisis and meaninglessness are growing features of contemporary experience. Many of the needs people express, or often find difficult to express, reflect a need for autonomy. It is just this – the need for autonomy – that I will propose should be the focus of political struggle. A fuller discussion of what this might mean for political action will be taken up later. For the moment it can be stated that such a politics will involve the need to loosen our dependence on capitalism. But, in saying this, we will first need to address the problem of the reproduction of the capitalist system.

The Reproduction of the Capitalist System

In today's political climate anyone who talks of the need to loosen our dependence on capitalism, to reduce capitalism's sphere of control, or even to dismantle capitalism, runs the risk of having their sanity questioned. There are many on the Left who might politely agree that the capitalist system needs to be replaced by a system that is more responsive to human needs but who decline to contemplate an appropriate politics for this task on the grounds that it is not feasible. Meanwhile capitalism drives on relentlessly, gearing production to the consumerist lifestyles of the affluent. In so doing it wastes life-supporting resources, increases pollution and intensifies ecological imbalance. The very existence, let alone the quality of life, of future generations is threatened. That threat is actually reality in the Third World.

Whole economies are shaped by the lifestyle demands of the advanced capitalist societies, while majorities suffer hunger, starvation, malnutrition and general impoverishment. In short, Third World lives are sacrificed for affluent lifestyles that promote psychic impoverishment. As a global economic system capitalism, at best, works in the interests of an affluent minority, and, in the long term, is not sustainable. But what of the feasibility of replacing capitalism with a better system?

If we are serious about the need to expand autonomy we will have to face the fact that this means, above all else, that opportunities for autonomy will have to be increased. Since it is the capitalist system that controls these opportunities by controlling key resources, the expansion of autonomy will inevitably involve contestation over resources – a contestation with the capitalist class.

> Things have come to the point where individuals must appropriate the existing totality of productive forces not merely to achieve self-activity but to secure their very existence ... The only way for individuals to control modern universal interaction is to make it subject to the control of all.[39]

Marx wrote this almost 150 years ago. It is even more relevant today, but most would say less feasible. If there is one thing that the capitalist system is good at, it is claimed, it is its ability to stifle its opposition. Somehow the capitalist system has prevented the development of the political will necessary to destroy it. The most influential explanation of how this occurs remains popular on the Left, and is largely responsible for the view that dismantling capitalism is not feasible. It is to this explanation – the dominant ideology thesis – that I devote the next chapter.

2 The Dominant Ideology Thesis

For most of this century, at least up to the early 1980s, the problem of explaining the ability of the capitalist system to reproduce itself was arguably the dominant problem facing social theorists and the Left. The problem was essentially conceived in the following terms: why, given widespread inequalities with enormous disparities of wealth between a very small minority and the vast majority, has the capitalist system not been overthrown by the majority? One must not see the problem thus stated as a concern peculiar to the Left and liberal academics. The recognition that class divisions might threaten the stability of the capitalist system was a constant fear of the capitalist class and their political representatives. This fear was clearly expressed in the lead up to extending the right to vote to working class men last century, as the following excerpt from a speech by Robert Lowe in the House of Commons indicates.

> The working men of England, finding themselves in a full majority of the whole constituency, will awake to a full sense of their power. They will say, 'We can do better for ourselves. We have objects to serve as well as our neighbours, and let us unite to carry those objects. We have machinery; we have our trades unions; we have our leaders all ready. We have the power of combination, as we have shown over and over again; and when we have a prize to fight for we will bring it to bear with tenfold more force than ever before.[1]

As we know, Lowe's fears have not materialised.

Among the explanations for the absence of a working class revolution the most popular and influential by far has come to be known as 'the dominant ideology thesis'. Essentially this thesis has it that 'modern capitalist society ... maintains and reproduces itself through the effects of a "dominant ideology" which successfully incorporates the working class into the existing social system, thereby perpetuating its subordination'.[2] In short the majority, who are dependent on the capitalist system for their survival, have failed to liberate themselves from this dependency as a consequence of ideological manipulation. Not only have the majority not developed the political will to dismantle the capitalist system, but they have actually adopted ideas, beliefs, values and discourses that wed them to the social system in which they are entrapped. Furthermore, according to the dominant ideology thesis, the manipulative effects of the dominant ideology are essential for the reproduction of the capitalist system. Thus Ernest Mandel claims that:

> To consolidate the domination of one class over another for any length of time, it is ... *absolutely essential* that the producers, the members of the exploited class, are brought to accept the appropriation of the social surplus by a minority as inevitable, permanent and just.[3]

Now it might be argued that the constant references to class domination that permeate the dominant ideology thesis give this thesis a dated feel. This is true if one links the working class with material impoverishment. But if the working class are defined as those who are dependent on the capitalist system for their survival, then quite clearly almost everyone is working class. While for a majority in the advanced capitalist societies this dependency no longer fetches up in severe material deprivations it nevertheless generates all kinds of insecurities and uncertainties. The dependent majority are always potentially vulnerable to the whims and fancies of the capitalist class. The prospect of loss of employment, for example, affects almost everyone in employment. Class domination *is* a defining characteristic of capitalist society. For advocates of the dominant ideology thesis, so long as capitalism exists the attempt to explain class domination remains highly relevant. It can be added that this relevance is not compromised by the existence of other forms of domination. Male and racial domination, for example, while often experienced as being of greater importance than class domination, are not *defining characteristics* of capitalist society.

What is the Dominant Ideology?

The concept of ideology is a notoriously elusive one.[4] By contrast the notion of 'the dominant ideology' is far more specific. Even so it is not that easy to pin down. Nicholas Abercrombie *et al.*, in their detailed analysis of the dominant ideology, define it in terms of dominant ideas that serve the interests of the capitalist class, and those ideas that reflect the particular values of the capitalist class.[5] Thus Abercrombie *et al.* refer to the ideologies of accumulation – those ideas that help to justify profit; managerial ideology – ideas that justify income inequality and socioeconomic status; ideologies of state neutrality and welfare – ideas that legitimate the authority of the state and the system of liberal democracy; plus particular elements of bourgeois culture that encourage a respect for hierarchy and deference to authority, and that promote individualism and nationalism.

Each of the ideologies may embody a vast range of ideas that contribute in some way to the reasonableness of the particular ideology, which in turn helps to make the subordination of the working class to the capitalist class appear reasonable, fair and just. An example will help to illustrate what I mean here, and will also help to demonstrate the complexity of the dominant ideology in terms of its multi-layered nature, and in the weird and wonderful way in which it works.

The idea that the education system is part of the opportunity structure contributes to the ideology of state neutrality. The idea that school achievement is related to future socioeconomic status, and the belief that it should be, supports the idea that there is, and should be, a meritocracy – the idea that rewards and social status reflect an individual's merit. The idea of merit, in this context, refers to a combination of 'ability' and effort. In so far as ability refers to a natural quality, an individual's position in the meritocracy may support the idea that it reflects a natural state of affairs. On the other hand the idea of merit may trade on the ideology of individualism – how individuals fare is essentially due to their own efforts. Either way the idea of meritocracy helps to justify divisions between employers and employees, managers and workers, leaders and followers, which in turn helps to legitimate the structures of inequality.

Obviously the state in the advanced capitalist societies is far from neutral. Its primary purpose is to establish and maintain the best possible conditions for profit-making. The dominant ideology is part of such conditions. We have already seen how the idea of meritocracy is interwoven with other ideas that are part of the dominant ideology. But if we dig a little deeper we find that the idea of meritocracy is even more ideological than I have portrayed it thus far. In particular we find that the education system, a major ideological agency involved in the production and reproduction of the idea of meritocracy, has ideological mechanisms to promote the idea of its own neutrality.

The capitalist system's main requirement of the education system is that it delivers young people to fit the labour market. Essentially this means that the education system has to have a mechanism for sorting out potential recruits for various positions of higher socioeconomic status from those, the vast majority, that are to form, ideally, a compliant labour force prepared to take up low-paid, deskilled work. The principal means for bringing this about is the examination system. Credence is given to the idea of meritocracy if the examination system is the one standard by which everyone's merit is measured, and if the measurements are deemed to be objective.

The apparently fair examination system that is open to all generates consequences that provide the idea of merit with a strong ideological flavouring. In schools all those activities relevant to the examination system are given a higher status than those that are not. This means that certain abilities and skills are more highly valued than others. But more than this, what is examinable tends to be so alien to the interests and experience of the vast majority that examination success involves overcoming this alienation. Those who manage this do so by developing appropriate attitudes combined with a fair measure of self-discipline which, in the context of schooling, means self-alienation. So, the idea of merit embodies a large attitudinal component, and it is this component that is reflected in examination success. It is this component, too, that is most relevant to employers.[6]

Attitude formation and self-alienation are well underway before children enter school. It is hardly surprising that those who have developed attitudes that are compatible with the cultural ethos of the school will find success easier to come by than those from social backgrounds that do not easily connect with school culture. Thus Pierre Bourdieu writes that

> our own pedagogical tradition is in fact, despite external appearances of irreproachable equality and universality, only there for the benefit of pupils who are in the *particular position* of possessing a cultural heritage conforming to that demanded by the school.[7]

The cultural fit between home and school is an important influence in shaping the child's attitude toward school, and teachers' attitudes toward the child, which in turn have a powerful bearing on scholastic success and failure. Early experiences of failure in school tend to be reflected in the child's limited expectations of future success and ultimately future prospects. From this kind of experience the school-leaver enters the labour market with a compliance that appears to be self-imposed. The education system, by producing and practising meritocratic ideology, has done its job for the capitalist system.

From the discussion so far it can be seen that 'equal opportunity', the official, neutral rule under which state-provided schooling is said to operate, is a myth. While most children attend state schools the opportunities offered come in a cultural package which favours children from a higher socioeconomic status. The ideologies of equal opportunity and meritocracy are mutually reinforcing. But the work of ideology does not end here. The apparent neutrality of meritocracy is promoted by yet another ideology – the ideology of IQ. Quite simply the 'ability' component of merit is assumed to embody general intelligence, and it is further assumed that intelligence can be *scientifically* measured. Within these assumptions 'merit' is given a scientific status, and with it the attributes of 'objectivity', 'truth' and 'neutrality'. In a sense the authority of science is enlisted to encourage the belief that the meritocracy is neutral and fair. Needless to say it has been easy to demonstrate that intelligence tests are culturally biased in much the same way as criteria for scholastic achievement.[8]

Much more can be noted about the ways in which the idea of meritocracy is ideologically constructed in a form that serves the interests of the capitalist system. Enough has been said, however, to illustrate some of the complexity of the dominant ideology.

How Does the Dominant Ideology Work?

We have already begun to see how the dominant ideology works. In particular we have seen how dominant ideas are materialised in institutional practices. The idea that the dominant ideology is embodied in, conveyed by, and transmitted through material practices is central to the renditions of the dominant ideology thesis advanced by Louis Althusser and Antonio Gramsci – the two theorists who have been most influential in the popularity of the dominant ideology thesis. They placed emphasis on the fact that social reality is infused with the dominant ideology. And, since we live our social reality, it can be said that the dominant ideology is lived. For Gramsci the dominant ideology structures and permeates all of our institutions and acts like a cement in integrating and binding society. Althusser identified a number of institutions, such as schools, churches, the family, the mass media, the legal system and the political system, which together make up what he refers to as 'the ideological state apparatus'. He singles out the school as being the most ideologically powerful of these institutions:

> It takes children from every class at infant-school age, and then for years, the years in which the child is most 'vulnerable' ... it drums into them ... a certain amount of 'know-how' wrapped in the ruling ideology or simply the ruling ideology in its pure state.[9]

He goes on to note how, at particular ages, 16, 18, 21, the education system ejects groups on to the labour market. 'Each mass ejected *en route* is practically provided with the ideology which suits the role it has to fulfil in class society.'[10]

In emphasising the material basis of ideology, both Gramsci and Althusser provide the dominant ideology with a *power* that is inconceivable if we treat ideology solely as a system of ideas that are explicitly communicated, as in the tabloid press for example. This does not mean that they ignore the ideas element of the dominant ideology. Althusser handles it by referring to it as 'the imaginery representation of the real world'.[11] More specifically he proposes that 'ideology is a "representation" of the imaginary relationship of individuals to their real conditions of existence'.[12] And, he further assumes that this enables the smooth reproduction of the capitalist system. This happens, as Gramsci puts it, in a way 'in which the individual can govern himself without his self-government thereby entering into conflict with political society – but rather becoming its normal continuation, its organic complement'.[13]

So, the dominant ideology works on people in such a way that they control themselves on behalf of the capitalist system. The most basic effect of the dominant ideology, according to Althusser, is for the individual to view him/herself as 'a free subjectivity, a centre of initiatives, author of and responsible for its actions'.[14] It is this that enables individuals to 'work by themselves', but since it is the dominant ideology that has created them as subjects, they are working by themselves for the capitalist system. In fact, Althusser claims, the individual becomes 'a subjected being, who submits to a higher authority, and is therefore stripped of all freedom except that of freely accepting his submission'.[15] Similarly Gramsci refers to 'the "spontaneous" consent given by the great masses of the population to the general direction imposed on social life by the dominant fundamental group ... '[16]

Both Gramsci and Althusser attribute an enormous power to the dominant ideology, and see it as the major obstacle to the development of socialism in place of capitalism. Althusser does refer to class struggle – but even revolutionary agents are, for him, ideologically constituted, not by the dominant ideology, but by revolutionary ideology. The precise ways in which the ideological constitution of subjects occurs is somewhat complex.

Althusser refers us to the psychoanalytic writings of Jacques Lacan, in which the illusions we hold with respect to our autonomy arise from failings of consciousness, which are themselves the product of the workings of the unconscious.[17]

For Gramsci the hegemony of the ruling class, in which ideology plays a crucial role, is never complete. It is something that must be actively maintained by the ruling class through cultural, moral and political leadership, and a measure of coercion. Thus the consent of the subordinate to their rulers is never automatic. Indeed Gramsci believes that the subordinate have a 'dual' consciousness, one derived from their own lived experience, and the other from the dominant ideology. The task of the ruling class is to attempt to ensure that the former corresponds to the latter. The task of the Left is to adopt counter-hegemonic strategies, part of which is ideological struggle.

Since, for Gramsci, the dominant ideology is considered to be dynamic rather than static, we are alerted to possible changes of emphasis within the dominant ideology. The pioneering work of Stuart Hall has been influential in this regard.[18] Hall has charted the drift to the Right in British politics and, as part of this, what he refers to as 'Thatcher's hegemonic project'. He argues that discourses of the Right emerged to address the moral panics of the 1960s. These panics revolved around observable trends in youth culture, such as sexual permissiveness, drug abuse, violence and indiscipline in general.

Eventually these concerns, Hall argues, led to the recognition of the need to re-establish authority, a need to which the discourses of the Right were better adapted than the more libertarian discourses of the Left. As it turned out the discourses of law and order became prominent, became part of the dominant ideology, and were materialised in repressive state practices. Given that Gramsci insisted that a widespread belief in the neutrality of the state was vital for the success of the hegemonic struggles of dominant groups, Hall's work demonstrates how the Right's ideological work was necessary to support this belief. But it also shows that under the coercive thrust of the repressive state, the Right were attempting to shift the state to the right, while attempting to promote the belief in state neutrality by means of a vigorous ideological crusade.

Is the Dominant Ideology Effective?

When Gramsci talks of the working class controlling themselves on behalf of the ruling class, he is alluding to the effectiveness of the dominant ideology. The absence of the revolution predicted by Marx, and the stability of the capitalist system, it is assumed, arises from the working class's adoption of the dominant ideology. Can this assumption be supported?

Prior to addressing this question it is necessary to alert the reader to two distinct ways in which the

concept of class is used. In the original formulations of
the dominant ideology thesis reference to the working
class is a reference to the vast majority of people who
are directly or indirectly dependent on the capitalist
system for their own survival. It will be important for
arguments developed later in this volume that this
'structural' concept of class is retained. In more recent
times, however, the term 'working class' has taken on a
more restrictive, 'cultural' meaning, referring to people
of lower socioeconomic status. Much, but not all, of
the evidence drawn on to test the dominant ideology
thesis tends to adopt this more culturally relevant concept of class. Distinctions are made, for example,
between working class and middle class subordinates.
Throughout this chapter I shall follow the usage of
'class' present in studies used to test the dominant
ideology thesis. There will be occasions, too, in future
chapters, when it will be convenient to refer to 'the
working class' in its cultural sense.

So, do the working class, that is people of lower
socioeconomic status, adopt the dominant ideology?
Abercrombie *et al.* sought to answer this question by
examining the empirical studies conducted on the beliefs
and values of the working class relevant to the ideologies
of accumulation, managerialism, state neutrality and welfare, and elements of bourgeois culture. For those on the
Left who are convinced that the working class have
adopted the dominant ideology the evidence does provide some support. Thus while the data suggest that the
working class reject the ideologies of accumulation by
declaring widespread opposition to large profits and their
unequal distribution, there is little evidence to indicate
opposition to the principles underlying the capital–labour
relation. Similarly there is clear evidence that the working class reject managerial ideology in so far as very few
go along with the idea that managers and workers work
together sharing the same interests, or that the consulta-
tion of workers represents effective workers' democracy.
The professional competence of managers, too, is
seriously questioned by a majority of the working class.
This and other data point to widespread dissatisfaction

among the working class with respect to the operation of meritocratic principles. But the evidence does indicate strong support for the meritocratic principles themselves. There is also widespread dissatisfaction with the operations of liberal democracy and the welfare state. Almost everyone feels that the political system is insufficiently responsive to their needs. Very few believe that the state is neutral. However, the dissatisfactions do not reach that point where there is a clear recognition of the fundamental contradictions between capitalism and the welfare state, and between capitalism and democracy. The veiling of these contradictions, it could be argued, is a deeply embedded feature of the dominant ideology.

Appropriate data on whether or not the working class have adopted elements of bourgeois ideology are hard to come by. Rejection of the idea that people should display deference to authority tends to be more a rejection of unpalatable ways in which authority is exercised rather than a rejection of authority as such. Although most of the evidence suggests that the ideology of individualism has not made much headway in working class culture, recent trends in the development of consumer-based lifestyles remain open to the interpretation that this ideology is increasingly influential. Even more awkward is the data on nationalistic ideologies – support or rejection of nationalism tends to be dependent on what nationalism is taken to mean.

As I noted earlier the dominant ideology is multi-layered. Generally the deeper layers have been widely viewed as more influential than the surface expressions, such as propaganda. The deeper layers are often unexpressed, operate 'behind our backs' so to speak, and constitute part of our taken-for-granted and unchallenged assumptions. The empirical evidence does suggest that the working class have adopted the deeper layers of the dominant ideology, that is, the principles underpinning the capitalist system. How important this is for the reproduction of the capitalist system is a separate issue, and one that I shall take up shortly.

Some might argue that I have made too much of the multi-layered nature of the dominant ideology, and that in doing so I have offered a distorted interpretation of the data relevant to the beliefs and values of the working class. A more popular interpretation is the one that Abercrombie *et al*. advance. They conclude that 'value dissensus can be found throughout the working class and concerns, in varying degrees, most of the range of ideological elements'.[19] More recently John Thompson has arrived at a similar conclusion:

> It cannot be plausibly assumed that there is a core set of values and beliefs which are widely shared and firmly accepted by individuals in modern industrial societies, and which thereby bind individuals to a common normative framework, for it seems likely that most core values and beliefs are contested and that there is a fairly high degree of disagreement and disaffection. If social reproduction were dependent on a generalized acceptance of core values and beliefs, then the ongoing reproduction of the social order would seem very improbable indeed.[20]

It might seem that we have got two opposing interpretations of the data relevant to the acceptance or otherwise of the dominant ideology. Can the interpretations of Abercrombie *et al*. and Thompson form the basis of a rejection of the dominant ideology thesis? The simple answer is 'yes'. This is so in spite of the apparent acceptance by the vast majority of the underlying ideological principles of the capitalist system. In order to explain this seemingly obvious contradiction it will be necessary to consider the role of the dominant ideology in the *reproduction* of the capitalist system.

The Dominant Ideology and the Reproduction of the Capitalist System

As I noted earlier advocates of the dominant ideology thesis not only assume that the working class accepts the dominant ideology, they also assume that it is the acceptance of the dominant ideology that enables the capitalist system to be reproduced. The dominant ideology thesis then attributes an enormous power to the dominant ideology. If the dominant ideology is to play such a key role in securing the reproduction of the capitalist system, it is clear that the acceptance of the dominant ideology must be a strong one. This is the problem for those who want to maintain that the working class do accept the core principles of the dominant ideology. There is very little evidence at all to suggest that the working class *firmly* accept these core principles. Firm acceptance of the dominant ideology, something akin to a commitment to it, is more regularly found among middle class subordinates.[21] The full implications of this commitment, *and* the lack of commitment to the dominant ideology from the working class, has yet to be grasped by the Left and social theorists alike. The major reason for this, as I see it, is that those who reject the dominant ideology thesis do so on the basis of considerations of there being an *ideological dissensus*. They tend to ignore those issues that arise from considerations of *ideological commitment*.

Ideological Dissensus

For some the existence of ideological dissensus is taken to mean that there is no dominant ideology.[22] Although this view is typically associated with the Right, it has become popular among some who claim to have leftish sympathies. It is a view that is compatible with characterisations of postmodernity that emphasise that 'grand narratives' such as Marxism and liberalism, together with other grand narratives, no longer hold sway. The dominant ideology as a grand narrative, in this thinking, is thus no longer dominant. It takes its place alongside other mini-narratives, ideologies, discourses or symbolic systems.

It is fair to say that there are considerably more ideas around today than there were just 40 years or so ago. But to claim that there is no longer a cluster of ideas that we might call the dominant ideology is to stretch the bounds of credibility. The dominant ideology is not dominant because a majority have adopted it, or even most of it. It is dominant in two senses. First, the values and beliefs of members of dominant groups are dominant, not by virtue of their appeal to the majority but simply because members of dominant groups occupy positions of power that enable them to enact their values and beliefs. The consequent materialisation of dominant ideas forms the material context in which everybody lives, and shapes the ideological climate. Second, some ideas are dominant in the sense that they serve the interests of dominant groups, irrespective of whether or not they are actually held by dominant groups.[23] In these two senses, if anything, the dominant ideology, within the context of a proliferation of ideas, has become even more dominant. One has only to think of the way in which the idea of 'accountability' has been tied into developments in the ideology of managerialism, and enacted in services such as health and education, to appreciate that the dominant ideology is alive and kicking. More than this, as the subordination of women and ethnic minorities has gained in publicity, a strong case can be made for the existence of an expanding dominant ideology – one that embraces myths about women and race. This expansion of the dominant ideology is particularly noticeable in instances when the demands of women and ethnic minorities are in conflict with the state's commitment to capitalism.[24]

We can also say that the dominant ideology has become more dominant throughout this century in the sense that its representation in symbolic forms has had increasing exposure through the expansion of mass communications. Obviously the mass media are far more than transmitters of the dominant ideology, and they may occasionally give expression to alternative and even oppositional viewpoints. However most media theorists are agreed that the mass media do, for the most part, convey the dominant ideology.[25] Sometimes they are actually compelled to do so by the state, as for example is the case in the British media's coverage of events in the north of Ireland. In fact the increasing intervention of the state, either to exert direct control, or to clear the way for the free reign of market forces, in both the mass media and in education, is clear evidence of the state's continuing commitment to ideological manipulation.

If there is no dominant ideology what are we to call all those ideas that serve the interests of the capitalist system, and those ideas that justify all relations of domination and subordination? If the ideas of dominant groups are not dominant how are we to account for those forms of institutional discrimination that deter the expression of oppositional viewpoints? Why, for example, do schools not teach working class pupils how to conduct effective industrial action?

Those whose critique of the dominant ideology thesis is based on an emphasis on the existence of ideological dissensus do retain some notion of ideological power. For those who privilege the idea that a range of discourses, rather than one or two major ones, co-exist, ideological dissensus is either the consequence of any number of discourses working on individuals in ways that produce a diversity of subjectivities, and thus viewpoints, or alternatively, individuals use the vast range of ideas and discourses that are available to actively construct their own identities and viewpoints. Ideological power is either embedded in institutionalised discourses, or is conceived of in ways that give it a crucial role in organising experi-ence and action. What tends to be lost in these accounts is any consideration of how ideological power (or ideological dissensus) might be relevant to the reproduction of the capitalist system.

This cannot be said of Thompson's analysis. He, like most on the Left, maintains that there is a dominant ideology, but as we have seen he questions its effectiveness. Yet, in arguing that there is an ideological dissensus, Thompson points out the consequences of this for social reproduction. Dissensus is descriptive of a 'lack of *consensus* at the very point where oppositional attitudes might be translated into coherent political action'.[26] He goes on to conclude that the 'reproduction of the social order does not require some deep underlying consensus

concerning values and beliefs, so long as there is
sufficient dissensus to prevent the formation of an effective oppositional movement'.[27]

This is true. But if we leave matters here we may
still be attributing too much significance to the power
of ideologies in people's lives. Thompson understands
the production of an ideological dissensus in terms of
the capabilities of individuals for 'distancing themselves from the social processes to which they are
subjected, of reflecting on these processes, criticizing
them, contesting them and, in some circumstances,
rejecting them'.[28] People are perfectly capable of
making their own sense of particular ideologies and
responding to ideologies in their own way. Again, all
of this is true. But when Thompson refers to the idea
that 'rejecting one set of values and norms may
coincide with accepting another', and when he refers
to values and beliefs playing 'a vital role in endowing
individuals with the social skills and attitudes which
govern their subsequent behaviour', [29] he is reproduc-
ing an assumption that is crucial to the dominant
ideology thesis itself. This assumption is that 'values
are by definition beliefs governing action'. Michael
Mann refers to this assumption as 'one of sociology's
most sacred tenets'.[30] To this I would add that it is a
basic tenet of western thought. It is one that remains
deeply entrenched among the Left. Further it endows
so much that goes on under the name of cultural
studies and social theory with an importance it does
not deserve. If values and beliefs govern action, and
if the sources of values and beliefs reside in ideologies, discourses, narratives, symbolic orders, or texts,
then quite clearly the power of ideology lives on not
merely in the ways that I have already suggested (see
pp. 27–30) but also in organising the individual's
experience and action.

In actual fact, unless we refer to everything as
ideology (thereby trivialising the concept) ideologically
relevant beliefs and values *do not* govern action for
the vast majority of people. To be fair to Thompson,
he does occasionally hint at this.[31]

Ideological Indifference

The problem with the critique of the dominant ideology thesis that is based on the prevalence of an ideological dissensus is that it fails to challenge the idea that the vast majority of people are ideologically motivated. If people do not adopt the dominant ideology it is because, so it is often argued, they adopt elements of other ideologies. It has not occurred to most advocates of this view that people might not be ideologically motivated. It is one of the basic contentions of this book that the failure to consider motivations other than ideological ones has been, and still is, largely responsible for the perceived irrelevance of the Left.

Many on the Left are justifiably suspicious of opinion polls and surveys, especially when the findings do not confirm cherished left-wing stances. This suspicion has been fuelled by regular electoral victories for right-wing parties in spite of survey evidence indicating widespread public support for the policies of social democratic parties.[32] Those who are fixed in their ideology-centredness cannot make sense of this occurrence other than by declaring surveys to be useless. It is this ideology-centredness that prevents the realisation that people may vote for reasons other than ideological ones. How can ideology explain the not uncommon phenomenon of people registering, at the same time, their vote for a right-wing party in a national election *and* a left-wing party in a local election?[33]

Of course the survey data on values and beliefs relevant to the dominant ideology are misleading. They are misleading because they ask the wrong questions. If people are requested to make responses to questionnaire items reflecting the dominant ideology, or any other ideology come to that, we get ideologically relevant responses. If we then take these data as the main index of what people think we would be ruling out a depiction of people as something other than individuals with ideologically relevant values. Within the assumption that beliefs and values govern action, we get a picture of ideologically motivated individuals, irrespective of the particular ideological slant of these motivations. In this scheme of things contradictory responses to questionnaire items can be understood as reflecting ideological contradictions in the respondent, and these in turn may be understood as manifesting false consciousness, or some other failure of consciousness.

In order to avoid this kind of nonsense, and in order to avoid a depiction of the most subordinate people that insults their intelligence, we need to discover the total range of motivations, including ideological motivations, that incite people to act. Only in this way can we discern the relevance or otherwise of ideological motivations.

The kind of data we require are in short supply. What evidence there is suggests that among groups of lower socioeconomic status at least, relatively low levels of commitment to stated beliefs and values are very common.[34] There are strong indications, too, that ideological commitments are nowhere near as widespread as they would have to be to satisfy the requirements of the dominant ideology thesis. In fact there is little evidence to suggest that ideology is important in the lives of the most subordinate.[35] Ideological indifference would seem to be a more apt description than ideological dissensus to capture the role of ideology in the lived experience of the majority. This is not to say that working class people, and other subordinate groups, do not have motivations and commitments, or values and beliefs – they do. 'Doing my best for my family'; 'trying to achieve economic security'; 'treating others as I would like to be treated'; 'maintaining good friendships'; 'having time for enjoyment': these are the kinds of values that most people hold. But they hardly suggest ideological motivations. Indeed they are ideologically irrelevant in relation to the reproduction of the capitalist system. They are values that will remain relevant to people in a socialist society.

The kinds of values to which most people display some commitment tend to be of *practical* rather than ideological relevance. And what determines what is practically relevant is what is possible in relation to experienced needs. What Dieter Wellershoff tells us of life in post-war Germany remains abundantly relevant:

> The only problems that really mattered were those to which solutions could be found within one's own sphere of action and did not have to be sought via circuitous political routes or in some later transformation of society. Should one rent an apartment or build a house, change employers or wait for promotion, get divorced or remain together – these were the decisions that preoccupied people. Anything more than that, anything that was not manageable or 'achievable', was considered too remote.[36]

Obviously if people internalise the dominant ideology, that is if they make it their own, what is possible, manageable and achievable will be unnecessarily restricted. No doubt advocates of the dominant ideology thesis will want to give priority to such an interpretation of Wellershoff's comments. To do so would be to miss the essential point. What people do and think about are restricted not so much by ideology as by the availability of resources. The time has come to dispense with the dominant ideology thesis. For the Left in particular it is crucial to tune in to what matters most to people.

Too many on the Left still *assume* that the reproduction of the capitalist system and relations of domination and subordination *necessarily* involves the ideological manipulation of the subordinate to the point where they internalise the dominant ideology. Because the social order is being reproduced it is further *assumed* that the ideological manipulation of the majority must be effective. Under these assumptions the Left have immunised themselves against the empirical evidence that tells us that ideologically relevant ideas are not really that important to most people. Political energies are invested in some form of irrelevant ideological struggle, and intellectual energies are devoted to analyses of how ideology works. In their wisdom left academics claim their ideological analyses to be politics!

There are far too many on the Left who have over-estimated the power of ideology over the individual and in the reproduction of the capitalist system. As such they misunderstand why individuals do what they do, and this in itself guarantees a relation of alienation with the majority. In response to accusations that he has exaggerated the power of ideology, Stuart Hall retorts: 'That is because the left has never really understood that ideologies are ideas which organise people's behaviour and conduct.'[37] Hall is wrong on two counts. The Left has been and still is to a large extent caught up in the power of ideology precisely because of the assumption that 'ideologies are ideas which organise people's behaviour and conduct'. And this assumption is just plain wrong.

An adequate explanation of social reproduction cannot be based on the power of ideology. Due weight must be given to the way in which economic and state practices have a direct, *material* bearing on the motivations and actions of individuals.

3 The Manipulation of Needs Thesis

Typically the 'manipulation of needs' is understood as a reference to the power of the media and advertising in making us 'need' things we do not really need. A former president of a major advertising agency tells us that:

> When income goes up, the most important thing is to create new needs ... [People] don't realise that they need a second car unless they are carefully reminded. The need has to be created in their minds ... I see advertising as an educational, activating force capable of producing the changes in demand which we need. By educating people into higher living standards, it ensures that consumption will rise to a level justified by our productivity and resources.[1]

Obviously there is an intent to manipulate here. The advertising industry, 'the machinery of demand creation', Christopher Lasch argues, 'continually tries to create new demands and new discontents that can be assuaged only by the consumption of commodities'.[2] As such, advertising reflects values that are at the heart of the production process. A former chairman of a major store states that:

> Basic utility cannot be the foundation of a prosperous apparel industry ... We must accelerate obsolescence ... It is our job to make women unhappy with what they have ... We must make them so unhappy that their husbands can find no happiness or peace in their excessive savings.[3]

The basic utility of a product is often regarded as self-evident. Most of us would prefer to wear decent clothes rather than rags, to have a refrigerator rather than not have one, to live in a comfortable house rather than a hovel, and so on. To want these things

does not require explanation. But what of products that
have no basic utility? How do we explain 'desires' to
consume goods that we do not need? Does advertising
– whether in the form of the 'hard sell', or in the
display of affluent lifestyles on film and television, or in
the display of goods in shopping malls – shape our
desire to consume? Have our 'wants' achieved the
status, and thus motivating force, of 'needs'? These are
important questions, especially for those who are convinced that consumerism is the primary motivation in
the affluent societies.

It is fair to say that the language of manipulation
has virtually disappeared from contemporary explanations of consumerism. There are exceptions – the most
obvious being those explanations of consumerism that
depend on some notion of the unconscious.[4] As Bocock
puts it:

> Consumption has become linked with the erotic,
> with infantile sexual desires, at very early stages of
> development in western cultures for both girls and
> boys. These layers of early, infantile emotion and
> feeling are assumed to persist in adult consumers
> because they remain in the unconscious, and may be
> tapped into by advertisements, for example.[5]

When this kind of thinking is used to argue that consumer motivations are the product of advertisers'
manipulations, incredible and mystifying arguments are
generated. Consider, for example, Janice Winship's
analysis of an advert in which a woman is about to
drink a glass of Guinness:

> The ad depends on our knowledge that women do not
> usually drink Guinness – they are 'ladylike' (and cas-
> trated): it depends on the *difference* between women's
> 'lack' and men's plenitude – the full glass of Guinness.
> However, that difference is *disavowed* in the conden-
> sation of 'ladylike-Guinness': women can and do drink
> Guinness but remain 'ladylike'. But the future pouring
> of the commodity Guinness between the as-yet-closed

lips – the as-yet-'ladylike' lips – is also a metaphor for
the sexual act: man's penetration of the lips, the
vagina, which provides affirmation of women's 'castra-
tion'.[6]

Winship's analysis does trade on the theory of the
unconscious. There are a number of difficulties with
this theory. Given that some explanations of consumerism are dependent on the theory of the unconscious, it
will be necessary to point out these difficulties.

There are essentially two conceptions of the relation
between the unconscious and consciousness. One of
these conceptions is unproblematic, the other is highly
problematic. In the unproblematic conception the contents of the unconscious are always potentially available
to consciousness. In the problematic conception, the
theory of the dynamic unconscious, not only is consciousness claimed to be cut off from the unconscious,
but it is assumed to be controlled by the unconscious.
Since, in this view, the unconscious cannot be known
directly to consciousness, and since it is only through
consciousness that a theory of the unconscious can be
constructed, the very status of the concept of the
dynamic unconscious, working in deep and mysterious
ways, is placed in serious doubt.

This doubt is strengthened in the light of more
credible accounts of what Freud took to be evidence of
the dynamic unconscious at work. One kind of
evidence, resistance in therapy, can be more credibly
understood as the reluctance of the client to disclose
private knowledge (the contents of *consciousness*) to a
more powerful other, the therapist. A second kind of
evidence, slips of the tongue, rather than revealing the
unconscious, can be better understood as a product of
heightened consciousness, our ability to think of more
than one thing at the same time.[7] Dreams, the third
source of evidence for Freud of the existence of the
dynamic unconscious, can be less mystifyingly understood as 'destructured consciousness'.[8]

Repressed desire, supposedly the most significant
content of the unconscious, is assumed to appear in

dreams, slips of the tongue, and resistance to the psycho-analyst's suggestions and resistance to self-disclosure. If these phenomena are best understood in terms of conscious rather than unconscious processes, then the controlling power of the unconscious is a myth. Besides it is doubtful that *powerful* desires are ever excluded from consciousness. By the same token if we are capable of repressing a desire then it seems most unlikely that the desire in question could hold any significance.

All of the above criticisms of the theory of the unconscious are relatively trivial, however. The most pertinent form of criticism is that which recognises that the resources available and not available to the individual are of primary significance in explaining action. In other words action is best understood in terms of the indiv-idual's material power and power-lessness, rather than in terms of the contents of the unconscious or consciousness.

While the theory of the unconscious remains influential in some explanations of consumerism, it is more generally the case that the more popular explanations avoid its use. What is emphasised instead is consumerism as a symbolic activity in which an *active* consumer, with an understanding of the cultural significance of products and images, uses goods to create an identity. Consumer motivations, whether or not they lead to actual purchases, are understood in terms of the symbolic value of goods for identity construction. If to this we add the *assumption* that consumer motivations are sufficiently powerful to sustain consumer demand, and the fact that the consumption of goods is necessary for the reproduction of the capitalist system, we end up with an alternative to the dominant ideology thesis. Thus Bauman argues that:

Reproduction of the capitalist system is therefore achieved through individual freedom (in the form of consumer freedom, to be precise), and *not* through its suppression ...

To secure its reproduction, the capitalist system in its consumer phase does not need (or needs only marginally) such traditional mechanisms as *consensus-aimed political legitimation, ideological domination, uniformity of norms promoted by cultural hegemony.*[9]

Bauman not only stresses the value of consumer freedom for the reproduction of the capitalist system in terms of positively wedding the majority to the system, he also argues that consumption plays the role of:

> an effective lightning-rod, easily absorbing excessive energy which could otherwise burn the more delicate connections of the system, and of an expedient safety-valve which re-directs the disaffections, tensions and conflicts continually turned out by the political and social subsystems, into a sphere where they can be symbolically played out – and defused.[10]

As I noted in the Introduction, if *all* of this thesis is true then the Left might as well pack up. Any appeal to the populations of the advanced capitalist societies to reduce consumption, on the grounds that such a move is necessary to prevent ecological disaster and the impoverishment of the populations of Third World societies, will fall on barren ground. There is even less point in trying to convince people that their consumer desires are somehow false, and that consumerism plays into the hands of the capitalist system.

Fortunately for the Left not all of this thesis is true. What is true is that the total volume of consumption is increasing. There is no sign of consumer demand waning among the more affluent, and there is every sign that consumer aspirations are lurking to be satisfied among those who have yet to experience affluence. It is also true that consumption is necessary for the reproduction of the capitalist system. It is further true that some (but definitely not all) consumption 'has become an active process involving the symbolic construction of a sense of both collective and individual identities'.[11] But what is *not* true is that *consumer motivations* are rooted in the symbolic value of consumer products for identity construction. First consumer *motivations*, especially among the affluent, are not that strong. Much consumption, like television viewing for example, is conducted in a routine way which, by virtue of being routine, does not suggest strong motivations. Second, even if consumer motivations are much stronger than I am suggesting they are, they could not possibly have their source in the *symbolic value* of consumer products for identities – except perhaps for that small minority for whom the symbolic is everything, and unless contemporary identities are no more than surface appearance or superficial displays of an individual's difference from others.

If identity motivations are to be given the kind of importance required by Bauman's explanation of the reproduction of the capitalist system, then they must have their source in identity needs. Basic identity needs, such as a sense of security and a sense of significance, relate more to the development and maintenance of meaningful and satisfying identities than to the continual symbolic construction and reconstruction of identities.

The relationship between consumerism and identity, to the extent that it is rooted in the symbolic, is nowhere near as important as we are led to believe. This is not to deny that consumer goods are of symbolic value – they most certainly are. But what I am saying is that the symbolic is largely irrelevant to identity needs. Further, if identity is to refer to a relatively stable and continuous sense of self, then we must question the real value of consumerism for the maintenance of identities. Consumerism as an activity is promoted by its own internal dynamic that creates dissatisfactions with the promise of satisfactions. Thus the recently purchased item provides only temporary pleasure. It quickly becomes a taken-for-granted object, and the individual starts to think about and orientate himself or herself toward the next major purchase. If our identities are tied to consumerism, they will always be in transition and thus destabilised and unsatisfying.

Not only is the explanation of the reproduction of the capitalist system based on consumer freedom misleading, but there is also doubt, in spite of Bauman's claims, that it is in fact an alternative to the dominant ideology thesis. The emphasis on the symbolic is an emphasis on meaning. What things mean, and how things are made to mean, has long been the stuff of ideological analysis. Given that ideology-centred thinking still permeates social and cultural theory it is not surprising that many see consumption as the product of ideological power. Thus Bocock refers to consumerism as:

> the active ideology that the meaning of life is to be found in buying things and pre-packaged experiences ... This ideology of consumerism serves both to legitimate capitalism and to motivate people to become consumers in fantasy as well as reality.[12]

While it is one thing to talk about the ideology of consumerism as perhaps an important element in an updated depiction of the dominant ideology, it is quite another to assume that this ideology, as ideology, has sufficient power to motivate people to become committed consumers. I have dealt with this kind of thinking in the previous chapter and there is no need to repeat those arguments here.

In arguing against the attractions of consumerism, whether they be ideological, identity based, or both, I am rejecting explanations of the reproduction of the capitalist system that are dependent on some account of the pleasures that attend consumerism. These explanations, as I noted earlier, have dispensed with the idea that social reproduction is secured via the manipulation of individuals. Against this line of thinking I shall argue that fundamental manipulations are involved. In saying this I am not about to reintroduce arguments that involve conceptions of 'the masses' as pitiful, pathetic, passive and unknowingly deceived. Quite the opposite. The vast majority of people are aware of the manipulations to which they are subjected by the capitalist system. I shall refer to these manipulations as the 'manipulation of needs'. And I shall argue that the best possible explanation of the reproduction of the capitalist system resides in an analysis of how that system manipulates needs. I shall call this explanation the 'manipulation of needs thesis'. Prior to spelling out this thesis it will be necessary to make some preliminary comments.

The Reproduction of the Capitalist System

An adequate explanation of the reproduction of the capitalist system must be based on an accurate account of what this reproduction *necessarily* involves. In other words we might see the relevance of all sort of practices for the reproduction of the capitalist system, but only some of these practices are likely to be absolutely essential for the maintenance of capitalism. The identification of the absolutely essential is especially important for the Left, and others intent on dismantling capitalism. One approach to identifying 'the essential' is to consider what it would mean for the reproduction of the capitalist system to be disrupted.

The capitalist system is by definition one that is structured by class relations. The capitalist class exercises its dominance over the working class. While this remains the case the capitalist class will always have the final say, and the working class will be the subordinate class. So class relations in capitalism are relations of domination and subordination. The state, as part of the capitalist system, has all sorts of functions, but its main function, above all others, is to do what it takes to maintain class relations. What this means is that the state helps to maintain the dominance of the capitalist class over the working class, and helps to keep the working class in subordination. I say *'helps* to maintain' because for the most part this relation of domination and subordination is *directly* maintained by virtue of the fact that almost everyone is *dependent* on the capitalist system for their own survival.

To say that the vast majority are dependent on the capitalist system is not to deny that some subordinates are well rewarded. To focus on this is to miss the essential point. Our dependence on the capitalist system stems from the fact that it is this system that *controls the resources* we all need to survive. It is the capitalist system's control of vital resources that enables the capitalist class to do more or less what it pleases. In other words the capitalist class is relatively *autonomous* in relation to the working class. It exercises that autonomy in ways that force the working class to be dependent on the capitalist system.

Of course the capitalist class is not entirely free to do what it wants. It is restricted by the fact that capitalists are in competition with each other, that they are dependent on some, if not everybody's, labour power, and that they must sell goods. They are restricted too by the fact that some of the resources used in the production of goods are not limitless.

For the vast majority, the working class, the money that enables the purchase of goods comes through the sale of their labour power. Given that the capitalist class is dependent on there being enough consumers with sufficient purchasing power to buy the goods on offer, they cannot go around exploiting *everybody* willy-nilly. There is always the danger that the resulting deprivations would give rise to social unrest that might erupt in class conflict, impeding the smooth functioning of capitalist institutions. But this is where the state is particularly helpful to the capitalist class. The state will use its authority, with the threat and use of violence if needs be, against the working class. For the most part though, high-ranking state officials, as good servants of the capitalist class, will want to avoid the use of violence. They prefer to keep a lid on potential unrest and conflict largely through the provision of welfare benefits.

Nevertheless, in spite of some restrictions, the capitalist class is more or less free to engage in its primary activity – profit-making. It can leave the state to tidy up the consequences of the worst excesses of the pursuit of profit. The state, for its part, attempts to ensure that the relation between the capitalist class and the working class remains one of autonomy and dependence. This is not always easy. The threat of disinvestment emerges should welfare demands generate increases in taxation on profits. On the other hand the threat of social unrest and disorder emerges if welfare benefits are not maintained at an 'acceptable' level, and if taxation on the incomes of the majority is seen as unnecessarily excessive. In order to maintain the relation between the capitalist class and working class as one of autonomy and dependence, the state has to tinker continuously with the economy. In recent times, as major multinational companies have increased their power in relation to nation-states, much of the state's tinkering in the economy has expanded the autonomy of the capitalist class and heightened the dependence of the working class. Thus, for example, regulations concerning trading, safety at work and employees' rights, have been relaxed or removed in order to enhance profit-making. At the same time welfare recipients have been more heavily regulated, and, especially in Britain, laws that criminalise certain forms of workers' protest and mobilisation have been enacted. Also in Britain major state-owned companies and services have been sold to private enterprises.[13]

There are of course many other ways in which the state attempts to maintain the autonomy of the capitalist class. At one end of the scale the state may use military violence to enable capitalists to have access to vital resources, to support foreign governments facing potential revolutionary opposition, and to support counter-revolutionary forces in socialist regimes. At the other end of the scale the state organises the socialisation experiences of the young in the education system. As I noted earlier, the principles of meritocracy that structure the education system and govern its practices actually reflect the need to maintain the dependence of the working class on the capitalist class (see pp. 27–30). Whatever the resistances to schooling expressed by young people, almost all of them leave school with expectations that do not threaten class relations.

Enough has been said to indicate that what is essential to the reproduction of the capitalist system is the maintenance of the dependence of the working class on the capitalist class. The breaking of this dependence would signal the end of capitalism. Above all else the disruption of the class relations that maintain the capitalist system *involves the effective expansion of autonomy of the subordinate in relation to the dominant*. And what is essential for the reproduction of the capitalist system is the *prevention of the expansion of working class autonomy*.

The Manipulation of Autonomy

The task of identifying what is essential for the reproduction of the capitalist system is not yet complete. We must also ask: how is the reproduction of the capitalist system *secured* by the actions of the working class majority? We can recall that in the dominant ideology thesis, action is understood as being governed by ideas, beliefs and values. In other words all action, by definition, is conscious action (even if some argue that conscious action has unconscious sources), and since this is the case, it is argued, it is the consciousness of the working class that holds the key to understanding why they act in ways that secure the reproduction of the capitalist system. The rest of the story is by now familiar.

Of course it is true that action *is* conscious action. But consciousness alone does not enable action. There is a far more important consideration. Quite simply there can be no action unless the individual or collective has the resources to enable action. A person cannot engage in the action of eating, for example, if he or she cannot get any food (resource), regardless of the consciousness of that person. If we were made aware that somebody had no food we would not dream of explaining the non-eating in terms of the person's ideas, beliefs or values. This is precisely the first inclination of advocates of the dominant ideology thesis, or any other type of thinking that assumes that beliefs govern action.

The objection can be raised that I have chosen an extreme case to make my point. More often than not, it might be argued, people do have some resources that enable action, that action involves choices, and that choices are a reflection of values. My response to this objection is simple. The choices available to people are restricted by the resources that are available. This means that in explaining action we must, first and foremost, take account of the resources that are available *and not available*. This basic tenet can be illustrated by a brief consideration of television viewing. In almost all western societies television viewing is the dominant leisure activity. Yet among those who watch most television, it is one of the activities they are most prepared to give up for some other leisure activity.[14] While there are particular programmes that people want to watch, most viewing is experienced as not particularly enjoyable or satisfying. Why do people persist in doing something that they admit they would rather not do? Those who privilege the power of ideology in explaining action might answer this question, as some have, by way of reference to the limited intelligence of those who devote most time to viewing television, or even in terms of some personality defect. At best this is misleading. I would prefer to say that it is insulting. Those who most watch television – housebound housewives and househusbands, the poor, the elderly, the infirm, young children – share one thing in common: their range of action is restricted by limited resources. Of the limited range of options open to them, television viewing is relatively cheap, safe, and is not burdensome in terms of demands on energy.

The example of television viewing alerts us to the possibility that why people do 'this' (like television viewing) could well be because they do not have the resources to do 'that'. Drawing on ideology-centred and psychological explanations of action can be further delayed if we recognise that much of what we do is not of our own choosing. The capitalist system makes sure of this by controlling the resources we all need to survive. In capitalist societies most of the resources necessary for the satisfaction of survival needs are not immediately and directly available to the individual. To gain access to these resources we either *have to* sell our labour time to an employer (or to customers or clients as in the case of the self-employed), or be dependent on parent(s) or spouse, themselves dependent on employment, or submit ourselves to the rules and regulations controlling welfare benefits. We are all ensnared in one or more sphere of dependency. This alone is restrictive of our autonomy. And each sphere of dependence has its source, directly or indirectly, in the capitalist system's control of the resources necessary for survival. The exercise of this control is the most basic and fundamental way in which the capitalist system manipulates our autonomy. This can be demonstrated most clearly by considering how dependency on employment controls the individual's time.

The Manipulation of Time

Full-time employment for most people takes up somewhere in the region of 30 to 40 hours per week, spread over 4 to 5 days, for around 46 to 48 weeks each year, for 40 to 50 years. As Gorz states it, employment involves work as 'an activity carried out: for someone else; in return for a wage; according to forms and time schedules laid down by the person paying the wage; and for a purpose not chosen by the worker'.[15] A vast chunk of our lives cannot be called our own by virtue of the fact that it is essentially for someone else, not out of choice, but out of necessity.

All action takes time and is 'in time'. Autonomous action involves the individual in choosing what to do in her or his time. This presupposes that individuals have time that can be called their own. Of course we all have time that we can call our own, but as we shall see this does not add up to much. In addition to time in employment we have to spend time travelling to and from work. We have to spend time purchasing the basic necessities, filling in forms, paying bills, maintaining our houses, and so on. We have to spend time performing necessary domestic labour and, perhaps, taking care of those who cannot take care of themselves, like children. We have to spend time eating, sleeping and performing other necessary self-reproductive functions.

We all have to spend time outside of employment in doing necessary things – necessary because they are relevant to our survival. But how and when we do them is not entirely up to us. How we perform all those activities involved in necessary consumption is largely determined by income, that is, employment. We know this, and this is why we give priority to being employed. Thus time in employment determines when we eat, sleep and so on. The activities we must perform out of necessity, both in employment and otherwise, leave us with very little time that we can call our own – very little time, that is, for the expression and development of autonomy.

Furthermore, of the time that is left over after we have taken care of necessity some of it must address the need for rest, relaxation and recuperation generated by our participation in the realm of necessity. All in all, what free time we do have is heavily fragmented, it comes in 'bits and pieces'. As such its use-value for autonomous action is limited. Those who do have tracts of continuous free time, for example the unemployed, or the retired, tend not to have access to other resources in order to make full use of this time.

I have made much of the idea that the capitalist system controls the actions of individuals by controlling their time. And I have emphasised that autonomous action is dependent on the individual's control of time, even though time alone is insufficient – other resources are required. It is often argued, however, that subordinate individuals are able to exercise far more autonomy than I am suggesting. I am not denying this. I am merely arguing that what autonomy an individual has is, first and foremost, a function of the resources available to that individual, and that this, in addition to the resources not available, should be our first consideration in explaining action. Further I am arguing that in explaining the reproduction of the capitalist system we need to account for how the *expansion of the autonomy of the subordinate majority is prevented*. The manipulation of time, I have tried to show, is one of the main ways in which this happens. In order for the autonomy of the subordinate to expand to a point where the reproduction of the capitalist system is effectively disrupted, there would have to be a transfer in the control of key resources from the dominant to the vast majority. This is inconceivable without the subordinate engaging in collective action that effectively challenges the capitalist system's control of key resources. Many of the ways in which the capitalist system prevents the expansion of the autonomy of the subordinate have the effect of arresting the emergence of the need for collective action. It is precisely in the provision of resources enabling a *limited autonomy* that the capitalist system best protects itself against opposition.

Autonomy within Dependence

The most effective way of securing the reproduction of relations of domination and subordination is for the dominant to get the subordinate to act 'freely' in directions that pose no threat to this relation. The value of labour power for the employer resides in it being a source of profit. As such the relation between employer and employee is inherently, and objectively, exploitative, irrespective of how well paid the employee, and irrespective of how the employee experiences this relation. By enlisting the subordinate in minor decision-making processes, that is those decisions that do not encroach upon the employers' and managers' spheres of autonomy, and by encouraging employees to use their own initiatives within the tramlines already set by company policy, employers attempt to use worker's capacity for autonomy for the profitability of the enterprise. There is a sense, then, in which it can be said that in granting workers limited autonomy employers get employees to exploit themselves. Employees who eagerly exploit themselves on behalf of their employers become candidates for promotion.[16]

The limited autonomy granted to workers is limited because it is confined *within the autonomy* exercised by employers. Autonomy exercised within this confinement not only does not threaten the autonomy of employers, but it strengthens the dependence of the employee on the employer. Similarly the limited autonomy expressed in consumption tends to reinforce the consumer's dependence on the capitalist system. All sorts of commodities might be viewed as particularly useful in increasing an individual's autonomy. The purchase of a reliable car, for example, enables greater freedom in travel than dependence on public transport. But the autonomy gained, as is the case with other major purchases, for example accommodation, is one that increases dependence on the capitalist system – through having to make regular payments (hire-purchase, mortgage) for the debt incurred, and needing extra money to tax, insure and maintain the car, and to fill it with petrol.

The various freedoms commonly known as civil liberties, while not necessarily increasing our dependence on the capitalist system, do not nevertheless pose it any threat. If these liberties are used in ways that might threaten the system they are readily withdrawn. In such circumstances freedom from arbitrary arrest is a joke, and in recent years in Britain, for example, freedom of movement has been denied to striking workers, and freedom of speech denied to Sinn Féin.

The limited autonomy granted to the subordinate, whether in the form of civil and political rights, consumption, or in the workplace, is also limited in the sense that it is an autonomy granted to *individuals*. In the absence of an effective opposition to the capitalist system individuals are left to compete with each other for status and rewards. The competition takes place on a playing field that is marked out in ways that encourage individuals to pursue greater individual autonomy *only* in the limited positions on offer. Energies that could be available for collective opposition to the capitalist system – the only way in which a real expansion of individual autonomy can occur – are channelled into competing for positions of limited autonomy.

Obviously it is preferable to have a wider rather than narrower range of rights. It is preferable to have money to spare than none at all, and it is preferable to have limited autonomy in the workplace than hardly any. But especially in the cases of the individual consumer and the individual worker, the limited autonomy is exercised in ways which reinforce dependence on the capitalist system. As Herbert Marcuse put it, 'The existing liberties and the existing gratifications are tied to the requirements of domination; they themselves become instruments of repression.'[17]

This is especially true of consumer autonomy. The very expansion of consumer autonomy normally, that is for the majority, at one and the same time not only reinforces dependence on the capitalist system but actually reduces autonomy. Enslavement exists at the core of our most celebrated freedom. This is so because in order to increase our autonomy as consumers we have to sell our time, and in selling our time we are delivering ourselves into the manipulative hands of employers. Thus Gorz emphasises that *'People must be prevented from choosing to limit their working hours so as to prevent them choosing to limit their desire to consume.'*[18] To this I would add that much, though not all, that is taken to be an expression of consumer desire is no more than the consequence of the resources available and not available to individuals. With very little time that might be used for autonomous activity, what are people to do with income that is surplus to need other than spend it?

Autonomy and Meaning

My considerations of autonomy so far have been in the context of explaining the reproduction of the capitalist system. We have seen how the autonomy of individuals is manipulated by the capitalist system in ways that secures its reproduction. In the discussion to follow the concern with the reproduction of the capitalist system will remain, but I shall focus more on the significance of autonomy for individuals.

It is safe to assume that individuals seek more from
life then mere survival. The expression of grief following premature deaths in starvation societies could not
take its intensely emotional form if this were not the
case. There are universal needs beyond survival. What
people seek is a meaningful and satisfying life. But
what is meaningful and satisfying cannot be prescribed
for us. What is meaningful and satisfying for one person may not be so for another. Given that what is
experienced as meaningful and satisfying is as potentially varied as the total number of existing individuals,
the surest way this need can be met is for individuals
to control their own lives. In other words the need for
a meaningful and satisfying life translates into the need
for autonomy. And, as we have seen, the need for
autonomy translates into the need for resources
enabling autonomy, that is, resourced time. Potential
for autonomy is increased as a consequence of increases in the availability of resources to the individual.

Having access to all the resources in the world does
not, however, automatically guarantee autonomy. The
extent to which autonomy is exercised is also dependent on how autonomous the individual is. The more
autonomous the person, the greater are the chances of
making full use of the resources available. We normally
think of an autonomous person as someone who is
author of his or her own actions, their own person with
a mind of their own, and perhaps resistant to authority.
Evidence of our capacity for autonomy abounds in the
resistances to parental authority displayed by infants.
But the extent to which this capacity develops into a
critical and independent mind, an autonomous disposi-
tion and valuing of one's own autonomy, is largely
dependent on socialisation experiences. To become
autonomous the individual needs opportunities to exercise autonomy. In the early years this involves the
adequate resourcing of family and school environments,
in addition to social conditions that facilitate the child's
development of autonomy. The most favourable conditions are those in which parents and teachers are themselves behavioural models of autonomous persons, in

which they value the child's development of autonomy, and in which they provide continuous and consistent love and support for the child's self-expression.[19]

Given favourable conditions the chances of an individual developing a sense of significance with a sense of security are enhanced. Both a sense of one's own significance, and a sense of security in oneself (what Ronald Laing referred to as 'ontological security') are essential for the continuing development of autonomy. The importance of a sense of significance, which involves self-esteem, is stated clearly by Ernest Becker:

> If there were any doubt that self-esteem is the dominant motive of man, there would be one sure way to dispel it; and that would be by showing that when people do not have self-esteem they cannot act, they break down.[20]

As far as ontological security is concerned Laing observes that 'the ontologically insecure person is pre-occupied with preserving rather than gratifying himself: the ordinary circumstances of living threaten his *low threshold* of security'.[21]

A sense of significance and ontological security are vital identity needs, and as such play a crucial role in the extent to which an individual can experience a meaningful and satisfying life. Obviously a meaningful and satisfying life is largely dependent on variety and quality of experience. But 'the meaningful' is not automatically given. The material and social environment is full of *potential meaning*. In order to transform potential meaning into actual meaning it is necessary for the individual to actively construct meaning. The individual's self, as a repository of meaning, is the basis for constructing and deriving meaning from experience. Without a sense of security and significance opportunities for engagement and self-investment in experience are lost. The more we are engaged in, and invest ourselves in, experience, the greater the chances of deriving meaning.

To put it another way, the development of the autonomous personality involves the development of the self's resourcefulness, that is the development of intelligence, knowledge, creativity, skills and so forth. The greater one's resourcefulness (autonomy), the more one is able to make out of experience. Of course the development of self-resources is largely dependent on non-self-resources, particularly other people. Hence the importance of others for the development of our own sense of significance and security. But without a developed sense of significance and security the self's resourcefulness is not only limited but is turned inward. The self's resourcefulness (the basis of the self as a repository of meaning) is cut off from the potential meanings that reside outside of the self. Thus Laing notes that:

> If the individual cannot take the realness, aliveness, autonomy, and identity of himself and others for granted, then he has to become absorbed in contriving ways of trying to be real, of keeping himself or others alive, of preserving his identity, in efforts, as he will often put it, to prevent himself losing himself.[22]

The exercise of autonomy requires an autonomous self. The maintenance of an autonomous self requires the satisfaction of the needs for a sense of significance and a sense of security. The extent to which these needs are met will determine the extent to which the individual is able to interact with the potential meanings of his or her environment. Frustration of identity needs underpins the individual's experience of himself or herself as 'problematic', and propels the person toward self-absorption.

Individuals who are self-absorbed are not only cut off from a more meaningful and satisfying life, they are, in a sense, cut off from society. They pose no threat at all to the capitalist system – their concerns are focused on the self, not on the forces of power that have steered them toward meaninglessness. Opposition to the capitalist system does require individuals seeking to expand the sphere of autonomy, and this presupposes that these individuals have a sufficiently developed sense of their own autonomy. The question now arises as to how far the restrictions on the exercise of autonomy, imposed by the capitalist system, encroach upon the development of our capacity for autonomy.

Capitalism and the Autonomous Self

Marx wrote that 'time is the room of human development',[23] and thus argued for an expansion of the sphere of autonomy. This could only be attained by the shortening of the working day.[24] Since Marx's day, working hours have been significantly reduced and almost everyone in the advanced capitalist societies is better off. On the surface it would seem that people are enjoying a steady increase in resourced time, which, as we have seen, is vital for the exercise of autonomy and the development of our capacity for autonomy.

However, capitalism is a dynamic force more or less continuously changing both itself and society. Many of the changes that have gathered pace over the past 30 years or so have actually eaten into our increased free time and reduced the value of our incomes for the development of autonomy. All those actions we perform out of necessity in order to meet our survival needs take place in a social context. In the advanced capitalist societies that context is one of increasing urbanisation and pollution. As urban space for human habitation has become scarce, cities have sprawled and living space has become more expensive. As a consequence travel time to and from work and shops has lengthened, and a larger proportion of our incomes has to be spent on accommodation. In the context of the decline of public transportation, ownership of a car has become, for many, a basic necessity.[25] And, in the context of an increasingly unhealthy urban environment, additional resources for the maintenance of health are required. Most of these changes, and other similar ones, have come about as a consequence of changes within capitalism, such as the relocation of sites of production, the break-up of heavy manufacturing industries, the mechanisation of farming, and so on. Thus Gorz argues that capitalism 'creates needs by modifying the conditions under which labour power can be reproduced'.[26] Claus Offe refers to these needs as 'structurally imposed'.[27] They reflect the expansion of the realm of necessity. The apparent increase in resourced time brought about by the reduction of the working day and increased income is not what it seems. The costs of survival have risen more quickly than pay increases, and some of our time that has been freed from work has been reclaimed by the urban environment. Most families need more than one income to survive, which reduces the time available for domestic labour let alone for the development of autonomy. Women, especially, know this well.

Arguably the most significant change experienced in recent times in the advanced capitalist societies is that of the deskilling of work. Many skills and crafts have been replaced by machines – fewer workers use tools and more workers are used by machines. Most jobs do not tap the individual's creativity or intelligence. Deskilled work makes no demand on those capacities central to the development of autonomy. Not surprisingly it is largely experienced as meaningless, as boring and as a drag. As such it creates new forms of weariness, depleting the energies necessary for a meaningful use of free time.

Of course there are still some, albeit dwindling, opportunities for meaningful work, that is work that makes demands on, and develops, the individual's autonomy. For the majority, however, work satisfaction derives more from the social interaction and banter than from the work itself.

Even the professions are undergoing a deskilling in the form of deprofessionalisation. This is particularly true of those professions that are dependent on state funding. The state is more or less continuously seeking ways of reducing public spending while maintaining the appearance of providing services that 'better serve'. Deprofessionalising the professions has become a useful strategy. Low-level professionals have lower expectations of exercising professional autonomy, are thus easier to control and, importantly, cheaper than high-level professionals.

As human service professions have been increasingly subordinated to the logic of economic rationality their whole purpose has been undermined. Their purpose is no longer to contribute to the common good but to look as if they do. Professionals become mere functionaries of inappropriate bureaucratic management, simulating the service they should provide. The public are decreasingly served; they know it, and so do the professionals. Encumbered with futile bureaucratic demands, and caught up in irrelevant routines, the human professions no longer offer the kinds of opportunity for meaning and satisfaction that they once did.

Although it is doubtful that we lose our capacity for autonomy, it must be said that most forms of work do very little in the way of developing this capacity. As the need for autonomous individuals has declined in most forms of employment, individuals, understandably, look elsewhere for meaning and satisfaction. This has implications for socialisation, and thus for the development of autonomy in future generations. As time in work, and in the expanded and more pressured realm of necessity, is increasingly experienced as meaningless, the widely expressed 'need for time' can be understood as a need for a more meaningful and satisfying life. Basically there is insufficient time for most people to satisfy their need for meaning. 'Sunday fails to satisfy', Adorno wrote, 'not because it is a day off work, but because its own promise is felt directly as unfulfilled ... every Sunday is too little Sunday'.[28]

Meaning is increasingly sought in the private sphere. But even though this sphere allows autonomy, especially for men, it is a restricted sphere of autonomy – a sphere of under-resourced time. As such it is incapable of adequately meeting the growing burden of expectations for meaning. As Lasch observes, 'It has freed the imagination from external constraints but exposed it more directly to the tyranny of inner compulsions and anxieties ... '.[29] This does sound like a recipe for self-absorption, and thus the loss of meaning. Whether privatism takes the form of self-absorption, or of satisfying intimacy and meaningful leisure, or of the less meaningful but easily acquired pleasures of consumption, it is nevertheless a form of social and political withdrawal. People get on with their private lives while the powers that be get on with the important matters. The reproduction of the capitalist system is secured in privatism. Marcuse reminds us that 'the entirely premature immediate identification of private and social freedom creates tranquillising rather than radicalising conditions and leads to withdrawal from the political universe in which, alone, freedom can be attained'.[30]

The Manipulation of Needs Thesis

We are at a point where we can bring together the essential elements of the manipulation of needs thesis in a concise form. As a thesis intent on explaining the reproduction of the capitalist system its broader concern is that of understanding how the dominant capitalist class is able to maintain its power over the dependent working class majority. Why has the revolution predicted by Marx not materialised? Part of the answer to this question is to be found in the reasons why agencies representing the vast majority, parties and unions, have been ineffective in sustaining collective action against the capitalist system. I have hinted at some of these reasons (see pp. 12–19) but a proper account, involving as it does considerable historical detail, is beyond the scope of this book. Collective action, however, does involve individuals acting in combination with each other. Understanding why individuals do what they do is thus of paramount importance in explaining why very few individuals become oppositional agents. The search for this understanding is the central focus of the manipulation of needs thesis. The search begins in what is common to the *experiences* of the dependent working class majority living in the advanced capitalist societies.

Let us start with the essentials. All individuals

experience two basic kinds of need that are the basis of motivations to act. The first and most important of the basic needs is that of survival, and the second type is that of a meaningful and satisfying existence. This need is open to each individual's definition, and *can only be defined by the individual*. The achievement of a meaningful and satisfying existence is dependent on how much autonomy the individual can exercise, and this, in turn, is dependent on the resources available and the extent to which the individual's capacity for autonomy has developed. The latter is dependent on the degree to which basic identity needs are satisfied. Thus we can say that all individuals have a need for autonomy, for ontological security, and for a sense of significance (even though most individuals are unlikely to express these needs in these terms). Expressed needs for friendship, love, even dependence, and so on, reflect the basic identity needs.

Human action is primarily, but not necessarily entirely, needs motivated – some individuals do have strong ideological motivations. But experiencing a need does not automatically compel the individual to act in ways that satisfy the need. We are capable of tolerating a lack of satisfaction, even of survival needs, although there are limits. Nevertheless needs do permit degrees of satisfaction and can be variously satisfied.

We can *begin* to state the relation between experienced needs and action by drawing on Lucien Sève's theory. He argues that:

> what incites one to act is not the need in itself and in isolation but the extent and conditions in which the corresponding activity is able to satisfy it, in other words, *the relation between the possible effects of the act and the needs to be satisfied* ...[31]

Sève goes on to state that the individual's 'intuitive evaluation' of the relation between the possible effects of an act and the needs to be satisfied 'can be seen to be one of the most simple and universal regulators of activity'.[32]

However, the actions that can be taken are dependent on the resources available to the individual. The knowledge of resource availability enters into the individual's intuitive evaluation of what actions are possible, and thus what needs can be satisfied. Because we *have to* address our survival needs on a regular basis, regardless of how affluent we are, doing what it takes to satisfy these needs has to be given priority from time to time. Doing what it takes to survive involves the individual taking a course of action in order to obtain the resources to satisfy survival needs. This is the beginning of the manipulation of needs. The first element of the manipulation of needs thesis can be stated as follows.

1. *The basis of all manipulations of need resides in the capitalist system's control of the resources individuals require to satisfy their survival needs.*

This control enables the capitalist system to determine what individuals must do in order to do what it takes to survive. Employers determine who is to be employed, the labour time involved and the level of compensation (wages) for this time. Employment is not organised for the satisfaction of employees' survival needs. It is organised for the profitable production of goods and services. Consequently, much production is surplus to need. As a result Gorz argues that:

> A growing number of wage earners must work and earn *beyond their felt needs*, so that a growing proportion of income may be spent on consumption determined by no need. For it is such optional, superfluous consumption, which can be directed, shaped, manipulated according to the 'needs' of capital more than to individuals' needs.[33]

Thus the second element of the manipulation of needs thesis.

2. *In manipulating the individual's need to survive the capitalist system manipulates time. The system uses up*

more time than is necessary, thereby depleting the indi-
vidual of time for autonomy. This, in turn, limits the
value of income for the expansion of autonomy and for
the satisfaction of identity needs.

While the majority of those in employment earn more
than they need, they are unable to exchange this surplus for meaning and satisfaction. The surplus comes in
the form of money, and there are some very important
things that money cannot buy. Gorz argues that 'consumption and the money which makes it possible, only
have a tenuous link with the things that make people
happy: autonomy, self-esteem, a happy family life, the
absence of conflicts in life outside work, friendship'.[34]
Fragmented free time is more suited to consumption
than to the exercise of autonomy.

Time for autonomy is further reduced by the effects
of meaningless work, which generates the need for rest,
relaxation, recuperation and easily acquired pleasures.
These needs can only be addressed in free time. As
Adorno expressed it, 'the appropriation of alien labour
weighs on it [free time] like a mortgage'.[35] Additionally,
the capitalist system increasingly taxes the individual's
energies, resources and time by the expansion of structurally imposed needs.

As a consequence of the manipulation of time, and
the manipulation of resources required for the satisfaction of basic needs, the exercise of autonomy is
thwarted, and the capacity for autonomy is underdevel-
oped. Thus, the third element.

3. *The reproduction of the capitalist system is secured by*
preventing the expansion of autonomy.

The expansion of autonomy, as Gorz argues, 'encour-
ages people to become extremely critical and demanding of the nature and finality of socially necessary
labour'.[36] It is also vitally important for improving the
individual's quality of life. The underdevelopment of
autonomy reduces the possibility of a meaningful and
satisfying life. Thus Giddens notes that 'Personal

meaninglessness – the feeling that life has nothing worthwhile to offer – becomes a fundamental psychic problem in circumstances of late modernity'.[37] With little opportunity for experiencing substantial and enduring meaning 'out there' in wider society, individuals increasingly seek privatistic solutions to meaninglessness, often in the private realm. The private realm becomes an arena for satisfactions. But the under-resourcing of the private realm works against its consistent provision of satisfaction. As a consequence identity needs are increasingly exposed – individuals are propelled toward forms of self-absorption, which, in itself, is the ultimate form of political quiescence. Now we can add the final element of the manipulation of needs thesis.

4. *The capitalist system, in precipitating privatistic solutions to the meaninglessness and identity crises it has created, reinforces its own reproduction.*

Issues receipt

University of Plymouth Library

Date: Friday, November 19, 2004

Card number: 0021014169

Patron name: HALA OSMAN

Item ID: 9002444236
Title: Manipulating needs : capitalism a
Due date: 2004-12-10 23:59:00

Item ID: 9002944112
Title: Sociology / Anthony Giddens.
Due date: 2004-12-10 23:59:00

Total items: 2
Please retain your receipt

4 Privatism and Autonomy

The manipulation of needs thesis holds some important consequences with respect to how we are to understand cultural trends in the advanced capitalist societies. In particular it offers an understanding of consumerism, privatism, and the emergence of identity issues that differs radically from the developing consensus in social theory and left-wing thought. As such it holds implications for oppositional politics – something I shall address in the next chapter. Before then it will be necessary to focus on those cultural trends that are causing problems for the Left.

The developing consensus in social theory's depiction of cultural trends can be identified in the prominence given to a number of observations: the growing privatisation of life; the decline of traditional communities; the increasingly central role of consumerism as a focus of life, including the consumption of cultural products; and the growing significance of issues relevant to self-identity, including concerns with gender, sexuality and ethnicity. There is, too, a consensus of sorts as to how these issues are to be understood. What we find is the continuing influence of ideology-centred thinking.

The cultural trends depicted by academics are obvious enough for all to see. But to see most, if not all, of these trends in ideological terms is to bark up the wrong tree. The ideologies of individualism and consumerism are often drawn on to explain consumerism, privatism, the decline of community and contemporary identity construction. On top of this there is much talk of 'the symbolic', of narratives and discourses as being of significance in people's lives. There is more than a hint that people order their lives by the meanings they construct. With the 'tyranny' of grand narratives broken, it is argued, individuals have even more freedom to make whatever sense they see fit. It is as if a space has been opened up for individuals to assert their

differences, a space that allows 'the free play of subjectivities', and thus a psychological freedom. This is
precisely where ideology-centred thinking leads. This, of
course, is fine provided that it is appreciated that the
space in which individuals can exert their own psychological determinations (their psychological autonomy) is
restricted. It is a power-bound space.

We are, after all, free to think whatever we want.
There are no limits to imagination and to what is
possible within consciousness. Action, however, is an
entirely different matter. There are things we must do
out of necessity. There is no point at all in psychologis-
ing what is experienced as necessity. This is a message
that permeates the manipulation of needs thesis. Let us
first see what individuals must do under the compulsive
and coercive powers of the capitalist system. Ideology
and psychology are secondary considerations. As
Politzer argued:

> Psychological determinism in itself is not a sovereign
> determinism: it does not and cannot act except within
> the limits, so to speak, of economic determinism ...
>
> Psychology does not therefore hold the 'secret' of
> human affairs, simply because the 'secret' is not of a
> psychological order.
>
> As far as the fundamental orientation and organi-
> sation of psychology are concerned, it is the mean-
> ing of economics which is truly fundamental.[1]

Bearing this in mind we can turn to a consideration of
the dominant cultural trends in the advanced capitalist
societies.

Privatism

Elim Papadakis and Peter Taylor-Gooby suggest that 'the
dominant current in the political culture of contemporary
Britain runs from collectivism to individualism and
thence to privatism'.[2] If by 'privatism' we mean social
and political withdrawal or abstinence, and coupled with

this a central focus on family and domestic life, and/or
some form of self-absorption then the concept of privatism is sufficiently broad to accommodate all the major
cultural trends. Indeed some concept of privatism does
figure in a wide range of debates focused on particular
aspects of contemporary culture. Thus discussions of
privatism are to be found in the debates addressing the
emergence and expansion of the 'affluent working class',
in the debates on consumerism, on the decline of politics,
on the gendered public–private divide, on collective and
self-identity, on the disappearance of traditional communities, and on the ideology of individualism.

What emerges from these debates is that privatism
does not have a singular meaning. But if we take together
all the various meanings of privatism it becomes clear
that we can characterise all the dominant cultural trends
as privatism. This is the approach I shall take here.
Following Josephine Logan's analysis of privatism we can
identify three, not altogether distinct, types: 'mobile
privatism' as a focus on private consumption oriented to
the family and domestic life; 'self-maintaining privatism'
as a focus on day-to-day survival; and 'post-necessity
privatism' as a focus on self-actualisation. Concerns with
self-identity are present in all three types of privatism,
and with some qualifications they all involve a retreat
from politics.[3]

In saying that *the* dominant cultural trend is privatism I am acknowledging what some on the Left fear
most. The growing disinterest in politics, reflected in
the declining membership of traditional political parties
and trades unions,[4] together with an increasingly widespread tendency for people to place their energies into
private solutions to the problems they face, does suggest a loss of faith in collective and political solutions.
Privatism is seen as an obstacle to left-wing politics in
so far as it denotes a phenomenon that is antithetical
to the more universalistic concerns of emancipatory
movements. Lasch echoes the Left's fears:

> the hope of a remedial politics, a self-reformation of
> the political system, has sharply declined. The hope

that political action will gradually humanise industrial
society has given way to a determination to survive
the general wreckage or, more modestly, to hold one's
life together in the face of mounting pressures.[5]

The survivalist orientation of self-maintaining privatism,
to which Lasch refers, obviously gets in the way of
emancipatory politics. But self-maintaining privatism is
not everybody's experience. Indeed the Left is less
bothered about the obstacles to emancipatory politics
presented by self-maintaining privatism than those
posed by mobile privatism. The fear is that those
people caught up in mobile privatism are so firmly
wedded to the attractions of consumerism that they are
lost to the Left forever. Thus many on the Left are
persuaded that privatism is an irreversible trend
secured by the combined effects of the ideologies of
consumerism and individualism.

There is no doubt that the ideology of individualism is
particularly well suited to the capitalist system. A core
element of the ideology of individualism emphasises that
how an individual fares is essentially due to his or her
own efforts. Those who make progress through private
consumption are thus encouraged to attribute their success to their own endeavours, and to look upon those
who 'fail' as not helping themselves. If effective, the
ideology of individualism promotes an anti-cooperative
and anti-collective ethic. And those who do fail are
steered toward self-blame rather than toward directing
their frustrations and anger at the social system. As I
noted earlier (see p. 20) the increasing incidence of
mental illness does suggest that self-blame is becoming
more widespread. It may well be the case that the continuing experience of failure, of 'being unable to cope',
leads to a psychic vulnerability to the ideology of individualism. While this suggests that we should not rule out
the possibility of ideological influence altogether, it
would be foolish, given the critique of the dominant
ideology thesis, to let matters rest here.

The tendency on the Left to see privatism as an
extreme expression of the ideology of individualism is

essentially without foundation. Many feminists have argued that as a consequence of female socialisation in capitalist-patriarchal society, women tend to develop anti-individualistic values. Given the gendered public–private divide, women are more entrenched than men in the private realm. Yet, rather than fuelling the ideology of individualism, women's privatism would seem to have the opposite effect.

Further, as I argued earlier (see pp. 45–51), it is unwise to exaggerate the attractions of consumerism as being responsible for launching individuals toward a privatistic existence. All in all, the Left is unjustified in seeing privatism as an irreversible trend, or in adopting the view that privatistic individuals are totally lost to politics. As Giddens correctly observes:

> Privatism, the avoidance of contestatory engagement – which can be supported by attitudes of basic optimism, pessimism, or pragmatic acceptance – can serve the purposes of day-to-day 'survival' in many respects. But it is likely to be interspersed with phases of active engagement, even on the part of those most prone to attitudes of indifference or cynicism.[6]

If, however, we want the 'phases of active engagement' to become much more than mere phases, then we do need a better understanding of privatism. The manipulation of needs thesis indicates that such an understanding is to be found in a consideration of the powerlessness (lack of autonomy) of the individual in the advanced capitalist societies, and how this powerlessness generates a focus on self-identity.

The Problem of Identity

Privatism is doubly promoted by powerlessness and meaninglessness. In 1972 Rollo May noted:

> I cannot recall a time during the last four decades when there was so *much* talk about the individual's

capacities and potentialities and so *little* actual confidence on the part of the individual about his power to make a difference psychologically or politically.[7]

Almost two decades later Giddens observes that:

If there is one theme which unites nearly all authors who have written on the self in modern society, it is the assertion that the individual experiences feelings of powerlessness in relation to a diverse and large-scale social universe.[8]

The manipulation of needs thesis demonstrates that feelings of powerlessness are justified – they are based on actual powerlessness. For many the private sphere is the only sphere in which the little power that the individual has can be exercised. It is the only sphere in which many individuals can hope to make a difference.

Our lack of autonomy, that is our powerlessness, in the wider society leaves most individuals bereft of substantial meaning and satisfaction. Again, it makes perfect sense to seek meaning and satisfaction in the private sphere. But the very powerlessness that steers people toward privatism undermines the resource potential of the private sphere for delivering the meaning and satisfactions sought. The more this is the case, the more desperate the search for meaning and satisfactions becomes. Resources permitting, some may avoid this desperation by way of the substitute satisfactions of consumerism. Others, however, direct their search for meaning toward their own selves. The self, after all, is one thing that the individual can shape, and over which control can be exercised. What most writers on identity refer to as the continuous making and remaking of identities as a characteristic feature of contemporary culture, is indeed a search for meaning. The search for meaning through a focus on self-identity is, however, largely a consequence of the individual's social powerlessness.

Now, it might occur to many that in treating today's concerns with self-identity within a broader discussion of privatism, I am ignoring the inherently social, and thus non-privatistic, nature of self-identity. Self-identity does, after all, involve an identification of the self with others and a differentiation of the self from others. The search for identity, it is widely argued, has been prompted by the collapse of those collectivities, like the fragmentation of the working class, and the decline of traditional communities, in which identities were once anchored. On top of this a diversity of others are now on display, and this opens up new opportunities for self-identifications. So the search for identity actually propels the individual toward the social, and away from the private sphere. Such an argument has merit if we confine our concept of privatism to refer to the micro-social space of the private realm. However, privatism, in a broader sense, refers to a self-orientation, irrespective of where the self-focus is played out. A central concern with one's self-identity, in this view, is inherently privatistic. Individuals play out their self-preoccupations in public. And to the extent that this happens, it can be said that the social is infused with privatism. Privatism is both a retreat into the private sphere, and a retreat into the self.

Giddens tells us that:

> modern urban settings provide a diversity of opportunities for individuals to search out others of like interests and form associations with them, as well as offering more chance for the cultivation of a diversity of interests or pursuits in general.[9]

If this is the case, and I think it is, then why are so many of today's individuals, particularly young people, more or less continuously involved in constructing and reconstructing their identities? Is it, as Giddens argues, because they have no choice but to choose? No, the more obvious answer is that the opportunities that do exist for identity construction are, for many, not experienced as meaningful or satisfying. And this is *the* identity problem of current times. We need to be reminded of the increasing incidence of mental illness, and the proliferation of therapies as indicative of the fact that there is an *identity crisis* of sorts.

The problem of identity is not, as most would have us believe, one of finding an identity – we all have identities. The real problem is that of *finding and maintaining a meaningful and satisfying identity*. To focus merely on finding an identity is to focus on the self's difference from others. There are indeed numerous opportunities for people to assert and display their difference. An exclusive focus on difference, however, whether by sociologists in their study of identity or by the individual, leads to a superficial sociological concept of identity on the one hand and a lived identity that is superficial on the other. The individual's meaning, so to speak, resides in her or his difference. But we must ask: how meaningful is this meaning? Jonathan Rutherford gives us a clue when he states that the modern identity 'is never a static location ... It is contingent, a provisional full stop in the play of differences and the narrative of our own lives'.[10] In other words modern identities tend to be transient, and this alone suggests that they are devoid of enduring meaning.

It does seem as if many younger people today do flit from one superficial identity to another, changing their self-presentation via dress, face or general style. Georg Simmel's observations on urban life at the turn of the century have a remarkable relevance today:

> one must meet the difficulty of asserting his own personality within the dimensions of metropolitan life ... one seizes upon qualitative differentiation in order somehow to attract the attention of the social circle by playing upon its sensitivity for differences. Finally, man is tempted to adopt the most tendentious peculiarities, that is, the specifically metropolitan extravagances of mannerism, caprice, and preciousness.[11]

Significantly Simmel goes on to state that 'the meaning of these extravagances does not at all lie in the contents of such behaviour, but rather in its form of "being different", of standing out in a striking manner and thereby attracting attention'.[12]

The interaction of superficial and transient identities makes for superficial and transient associations, which in turn reinforce the experience of meaninglessness. Why do so many individuals invest their energies in these associations? The conventional wisdom in sociology suggests that this is actually what young people want! The extreme form of superficial and transient association is that offered by the mass media. Yet Dick Hebdige argues that the global media have the power 'to move people not just to buy the products of the culture industries but to buy *into* networks that offer forms of community and alliance which can transcend the confines of class, race, gender, regional and national culture'.[13] He refers to the mass media offering opportunities for participatory bonding, for example Band Aid, which create 'communities of affect'. Specifically contradicting observations that in recent times there is a 'waning of affect', and an increase in 'psychic autism', Hebdige suggests that there is a 'desire to feel and to feel *connected* to a transitory mass of other people', and 'to engage in transitory and *superficial* alliances ...'[14]

While the communities of affect, to which Hebdige refers, might provide enjoyment and fleeting meaning, it is doubtful that they are experienced as meaningful in any significant way. This is so precisely because they are superficial, transitory and disconnected from any interactive framework in which identity can be established and maintained. Of course there are many social networks that are neither abstract (non-interactive) nor transient, and they would seem to supply many people with sufficient meaning to help maintain satisfying identities. It may well be the case that the development of such networks is a growing trend. But it is also the case that there is an opposite trend: the retreat into the private sphere and the self. The private sphere offers the self that is seeking substantial meaning the promise of feeling connected to others in intimate and more stable relationships. But

the private sphere, being inherently restrictive, and
existing in a universe experienced as meaningless, often fails to fulfil its promise – it fails under the
weight of excessive expectations for satisfaction. Self-
preoccupations, in these circumstances, can be intensi-
fied to the point where the self becomes problematic
to itself. There is little wonder that therapy has become a booming industry.

Identity Crises

No doubt we all make and remake our self-identities. In
recent times, however, the manic and intense forms
assumed by this process suggest that for a growing
number of people the self is in trouble. The manipulation
of needs thesis makes it clear that the limited autonomy
available to individuals today creates conditions in which
there is a greater likelihood of identity needs being
exposed. Identity crisis is the experienced lack of satisfaction of identity needs. Individuals may well need to
'be different', and to express their difference. Of far
greater importance, however, is the extent to which
individuals feel secure in themselves, and experience
themselves as significant. Identity, Erik Erikson argues,
is 'not just a conscious choice of what kind of nice
identity one would like to have ... identity means what
the best in you lives by, the loss of which would make
you less human'.15 Erikson, quite correctly, points out
that there can be no such thing as a meaningful and
satisfying identity without it being anchored in a group
setting.

Work-based identities, as work has become increasingly deskilled, have declined in terms of the satisfactions they offer. Their replacement by consumer-based
identities has been far from satisfactory. As I have
already argued, consumer-based identities are inherently transient and destabilising, useful perhaps for the
superficial display of difference, but hardly relevant to
identity needs. Besides, consumption is *private* consumption, used perhaps for *symbolic* interaction, which

is a far cry from what it means to anchor one's identity in a group setting.

The changes precipitated by the capitalist system, which have brought about a shift in focus from work to consumption and leisure, have also brought about a decline in community life and unleashed processes of social fragmentation. Up to about the 1950s the vast majority lived, worked, shopped, went to school, and took their recreation in the same locality. Whatever the rigidities and limitations of traditional communities, they nevertheless did constitute group settings, providing daily face-to-face interaction that normally supplied the individual with some significance and security, if only in the form of having their existence confirmed. While community life could generate unwanted intrusions of privacy, it did provide protection from social isolation and loneliness. Community life did just enough to prevent identity crises, and to prevent the private sphere from being overburdened and pressurised to supply the kinds of satisfaction demanded of it today.

With the break-up of traditional communities, and with equivalent social networks and settings in short supply, individuals are thrown directly on to the private sphere, and are more dependent on their own resources for developing and maintaining a sense of well-being. Processes of identification and differentiation take place increasingly in imaginary rather than practical interactions – as in interactions with the electronic media, and with the projected self-images of others. The permanently present, real others of yesteryear, have been gradually replaced by the fleetingly present, abstract others of today. Only secure identities can handle this.

It would be too simplistic to single out the decline of community as a cause of identity crisis. As I have already indicated there are a number of factors working together to undermine the development of meaningful and satisfying identities. Mental illness – the end point of identity crisis – does have its primary sources in the total social system, and the growth in demand for therapy reflects this. As Wolf-Dieter Narr points out, 'Psychotherapy is concerned primarily with problems stemming from the fact that various social institutions now make use of individuals only in specific roles, systematically ignoring their needs.'[16] Not that therapy can do much better. By the time the despairing get to therapy, their ontological insecurity and sense of their own superfluousness can only be overcome by sustained, genuine love. Instead therapy offers a parallel version of the superficial relationships that increasingly typify contemporary associations. Therapy, of course, can be little other than a pseudo, professionally fabricated relationship. As such its distance from the interactions of raw emotions gives it an abstract quality, useful maybe for those not in need of repair, but also, because of its emotional irrelevance, an additional source of depression.

By comparison with community, therapy is not equipped to address the sources of an individual's distress. There is no magic talk or pill that can change social conditions. Therapists cannot prescribe revolution. They do quite the opposite. The individual, in therapy, is *the* problem, not the social conditions. It is the individual that has to change to adapt to inhuman social conditions.

As such, therapy is a tool of the ideology of individualism. Yet the demand for therapy will grow in direct proportion to the failure of the social system to provide sufficient opportunities for the satisfaction of identity needs. The increasing popularity of public confessionals on nationwide television – the latest form of therapy – both in terms of those queuing up to disclose the messy details of their private lives, and those attracted to viewing the distasteful spectacle, is recent evidence that the exposure of identity needs has become normalised.

While the better resourced may avoid crisis, it is nevertheless the case that obsessions with diet, fitness, appearance, sex, intimacy, psychology and so on, arise from preoccupations with identity needs. It is this, too, that underpins the trend of using therapy for 'self-actualisation'. The self-absorptions of those more or less continuously caught up in an orientation of self-management are no less privatistic. Privatistic transformations of the self, whatever the psychological benefits to the individual, are always going to be a limited form

western societies. First socialisation refers to processes which attempt to get, as Laing aptly put it, 'each new recruit to the human race to behave in substantially the same way as those who have already got there'.[18] Socialisation is thus centrally involved in shaping individuals to act in ways to help reproduce relations of domination and subordination. Thus Adorno noted that:

> The feminine character, and the ideal of femininity on which it is modelled, are products of masculine society ... The feminine character is a negative imprint of domination ... The femininity which appeals to instinct, is always exactly what every woman has to force herself by violence – masculine violence – to be: a she-man.[19]

We could not possibly refer to the socialisation of girls, or any other subordinate group come to that, as a process that culminates in autonomy.

More than this, and this is the second major issue, all socialisation, if successful, generates self-alienation. In other words, agencies of socialisation, particularly the family and the school, engage in practices directed at subduing and suppressing the individual's inclination for autonomous action. Individuals' energies, rather than being freely invested in autonomous acts, are diverted into responding to the demands of more powerful others, and into becoming what others want them to be. The more successful the socialisation, the better the individual is adjusted to society. Laing wrote that:

> the result of such adjustment to our society is that, having been tricked and having tricked ourselves out of our minds, that is to say, out of our own personal worlds of experience, out of that unique meaning with which potentially we may endow the external world, simultaneously we have been conned into the illusion that we are separate 'skin-encapsulated egos'. Having at one and the same time lost our *selves* and developed the illusion that we are autonomous *egos*, we are

expected to comply by inner consent with external
constraints, to an almost unbelievable extent.[20]

Social critics feared that with the agencies of socialisation all pulling together in the same direction, and with
more sophisticated techniques of manipulation available
to teachers, our capacity for autonomy might be
crushed. This fear was particularly strong among those
who associated the popular appeal of fascism with a
decline in the autonomous individual. Loss of autonomy
lowers the individual's resistance to authority and
makes the individual more vulnerable to the manipulations of others. Thus Max Horkheimer noted that 'the
impact of the existing conditions upon the average
man's life is such that the submissive type ... has
become overwhelmingly predominant'.[21]

Adorno, Horkheimer and Marcuse, each in their own
(though largely similar) way, from the 1930s through to
the 1960s, attempted to understand why the 'submissive
type' had become predominant. Of particular significance, they felt, was the declining influence of the family,
and the growing influence of external agencies in childhood. At the same time, changes in capitalism, from
entrepreneurial to organised industrial capitalism,
throughout the nineteenth century, they argued, had less-
ened the scope for the exercise of male autonomy outside of the family.[22] As a consequence, the father, as a
behavioural model of autonomy, was disappearing. This,
they felt, undermined the father's legitimate authority in
the family. Given that they believed that the development
of the autonomous personality was closely bound up with
the maturing child's resistance to parental authority
within the 'protective security' of the family, and that the
development of autonomy required sufficient time (often
into late adolescence) to satisfactorily 'work through' the
resistances to the point where parental authority was
internalised, they viewed the declining influence of the
family with considerable alarm. The internalisation of
parental authority, in this view, is the basis of the autonomous personality. Thus Marcuse argued that: 'Through
the struggle with father and mother as personal targets of

love and aggression, the younger generation entered societal life with impulses, ideas, and needs which were largely *their* own.[23]

But in the context of changes in the wider society, including the expansion of the state's jurisdiction in education, child rearing and family welfare, Horkheimer, writing in the 1950s, observed that:

> Today the child is much more directly thrown upon society, childhood is shortened, and the result is a human being cast in a different mold. As interiority has withered away, the joy of making personal decisions, of cultural development, and of the free exercise of the imagination has gone with it.[24]

Thus while Horkheimer recognised that the individual 'leaves the family a less encumbered person', the price paid for this was 'loss of the interiority that had formerly been developed during the interaction which went on throughout a long childhood'.[25] 'Interiority' is, in fact, what gives a person depth and substance; it is the basis of the individual's sense of himself or herself as an autonomous person. The satisfactions derived from the exercise of autonomy steeped in interiority not only increase the individual's resistance to authority but fuel a need for an expanded sphere of autonomy. Without interiority the individual's apparent autonomy is a superficial one; it is a whimsical autonomy providing no substantial basis for choices, no strong preferences and thus a 'take it or leave it' attitude.

With the external agencies of socialisation, especially the mass media, increasingly invading a childhood that no longer generates interiority, there is some justification in supposing that the child is even more likely to enter adulthood with less autonomy than Horkheimer thought. If this is the case it makes any politics aiming for an expansion of autonomy that much more difficult. Individuals without a sense of themselves as autonomous are unlikely to find such a politics attractive. Yet we know that *it is objectively the case* that a deeply entrenched sense of self as autonomous – entrenched in

the individual's ontological security and sense of significance – is the surest protection against meaninglessness.
Somehow this knowledge must become the guiding principle of early socialisation. Luckily the obstacles to this
are being removed.

Not so long ago, when a range of careers was available
to school leavers, and when there appeared to be some
connection between scholastic achievement and future
socio-economic status, parents could feel justified (often
against their 'softer' nature) in using their authority over
the child in ways directed at giving the child a 'decent'
start in life, a start that would hopefully place the child
on 'the straight and narrow' for future success. 'Getting
on' in life was equated with getting a good job, or
alternatively a 'good' husband. Most people had a shared
and clear grasp of what was meant by 'good' and 'bad',
and 'right' and 'wrong'. Allowing children the freedom to
pursue their autonomous inclinations was widely
regarded as potentially impeding their chances of 'getting
on'. Even though parents and school were pulling in the
same direction, the youth rebellions of the 1960s, albeit
involving only a small minority, began to challenge the
values of the 'good' society. The onslaught against
autonomy was not totally successful. Besides, many families have never found it easy to maintain their grip over
their children, and many teachers have always had difficulties in pacifying and controlling the young. Autonomy
might be under-developed, but its underlying capacity
emerges from time to time.

Recent changes within capitalism, however, have
opened up an enormous emancipatory potential. All but
a few careers have gone. There is no longer a clear
connection between scholastic success and future career.
Indeed the most scholastically successful are less likely
to find employment than their less successful peers.[26]
Deprofessionalisation and the deskilling of work are undermining the traditional direction of schooling. If
schools were seriously to address themselves to today's
labour requirements they would have to encourage
numeracy and literacy, encourage a minority to develop a
technical intelligence, encourage a majority to become

mindless automatons capable of obediently fulfilling prescribed, deskilled work routines, and discourage all from
developing a free imagination and critical intelligence.
Schools are clearly in an impossible position.
While schools remain part of the state machinery
they will be obliged to enact government policies. But
most of the reasons parents once had for repressing the
child's development of autonomy no longer exist. There
are no paths to follow that can guarantee future success. What does it mean to be successful anyway?
Parents are beginning to share in their children's disil-
lusionment, both with school and uncertain futures.
Economy, teachers and parents no longer tread the
same path, and there is widespread disagreement as to
what 'the path' is or should be. There are no longer any
clear rewards for blocking the development of the
autonomous personality.

In summing up the discussion of contemporary cultural
trends, it is clear that the experienced lack of
autonomy steers people toward the private sphere, and
can result in apolitical self-absorption. But there is also
a sense in which privatism can be seen to reflect an
attempt to exercise autonomy. We can take heart from
this because it means that our capacity for autonomy is
still alive. But more than this, opportunities are opening
up for the development of this capacity in the private
sphere. If this opportunity is seized future generations
will be better able to avoid self-absorption, and will be
less satisfied than the present ones with restricting
their exercise of autonomy to the private sphere.

5 Toward a Culture of Opposition

Even though privatism, as the dominant cultural trend in the advanced capitalist societies, does embody signs that can provide some hope for a future emancipatory politics, it must be admitted that these signs do not add up to much in the total order of things. However much privatism reflects the continuing existence of the individual's capacity for autonomy, it nevertheless reflects far more the individual's limited opportunities for developing this capacity and exercising autonomy. As we have seen these limitations enable the reproduction of the capitalist system. Further, a privatised culture is, in and of itself, an obstacle to the development of emancipatory politics. On the one hand a privatised culture – privatised in the sense of a life primarily focused on the private sphere – is an atomised culture denoting social fragmentation and isolationism. As such privatised culture poses a barrier to progressive forces of social change that are dependent on mass participation. On the other hand a privatised culture – privatised in the sense of self-preoccupations coming to the fore in communication and social interaction – suggests that what concerns individuals most is at a far remove from the more universalistic concerns associated with emancipatory politics.

The difficulties that a privatistic culture present for emancipatory politics have no doubt contributed to the declining presence of political opposition in recent years. And this in turn, in so far as it could provide individuals with a purposeful focus for their dissatisfactions, reinforces privatism. The longer this state of affairs continues the more likely it is that privatism and the absence of emancipatory political initiatives will negatively reinforce each other, thereby widening the gulf between individuals and politics.

It is against the backdrop of this prospect that political opposition must be formed. On the face of it, it seems an impossible task. Not only must political opposition to the capitalist system overcome privatism, it must be seen to be sufficiently effective to inspire hope. Ineffective opposition merely fuels privatism. An effective opposition requires much more than the odd protest, much more than a single-issue campaign of minority interest, much more than small social movements working in isolation, and much more than little radical political parties agitating over the major issues of the day. A political opposition can be effective only if it is a unified opposition. This means that oppositional forces must pull together, and it implies that there is a central focus around which they can pull together. Anyone with experience of involvement in oppositional politics will know just how difficult this is. Disagreements and differences between oppositional groups tend to override the need for unity and solidarity.

Something has got to give. That 'something' is what I have referred to as 'ideology-*centred* thinking'. No amount of ideological onslaught against capitalism, US imperialism, nuclear weapons, environmental neglect, patriarchy, racism and so on will have its desired impact unless it can be seen to make a *practical* difference in people's lives. In fact there is no point at all to oppositional politics unless significant practical improvements are aimed for. Oppositional forces, furthermore, are so committed to their particular viewpoints that ideological unity cannot come about through ideological debate. Ideological debate merely heightens ideological differences, retains a focus on ideological matters, and divorces the oppositional forces from practical concerns. Not surprisingly actions that emanate from ideology-centred politics tend to be symbolic.

We must break with ideology-centred thinking and politics. This does not mean that we give up our principles and our ideological commitments. It does mean that we background them in order to focus on what would most improve people's lives in practical, tangible ways. The manipulation of needs thesis, and the understanding of privatism that it provides, suggest that significant improvements in people's lives can be achieved by *expanding the sphere of autonomy*. It is the expansion of autonomy that I am proposing as a unifying focus for oppositional politics.

To propose this is to propose nothing new. The expansion of autonomy has always been at the heart of emancipatory politics. All relations of domination and subordination, whether they be imperialism, class, sex or race, are, after all, relations of autonomy and dependence. The 'emancipatory interest' assumes that it is not in the interests of members of subordinate groups to remain in subordination. Who in their right mind could claim that the prolonged experience of subordination is good for them? To be a subordinate means that one's life is essentially controlled by others. The others may come in the form of an individual or individuals, institutions or social system. To be liberated from subordination means to break out of our dependency on those others who control us. And to break out of our dependency involves the expansion of our autonomy. But the continuing expansion of autonomy can proceed only so far as an individual matter. There comes a point where the continuing expansion of autonomy is dependent on the dismantling of the institutional basis of forms of domination. This can only happen as a consequence of collective action. When this happens – that is, when individuals recognise that the quality of their own individual lives can only be improved by collective, rather than private, initiatives – we will have reached the point at which genuine democracy emerges. It is only through genuine democracy, that is collective self-determination, that most of the bigger problems, like global inequalities, world peace, ecological disaster and so on, can be properly addressed.

While it is a relatively easy matter to demonstrate that the expansion of individual autonomy is directly relevant to the various concerns of oppositional politics, it is quite another matter to translate this into practical politics. For much of modern history the expansion of individual and collective autonomy has been understood as involving an increase in the resources available to people. The dominant concerns of emancipatory politics have been: increasing collectively provided resources, for example energy, transport, health care; increasing collective provision of social opportunity, for example education; and increasing the resource of individual incomes. While two-thirds of the world's population suffer acute forms of material deprivation that threaten survival, life expectancy and life chances, the need for this kind of emancipatory politics remains. But with approximately two-thirds of the populations of the advanced capitalist societies no longer in *need* of more basic resources, there is insufficient support for an emancipatory politics focused on material deprivation. Further, the increase in the availability of resources to the relatively affluent two-thirds has been achieved at the expense of the impoverished in the Third World, and in their own societies, *and* without breaking out of their dependency on the capitalist system.

On the surface it would seem that an emancipatory politics focused on the expansion of autonomy that leads to the dismantling of the capitalist system has no chance of taking off in the advanced capitalist societies. Even though the capitalist system regularly harms small minorities within the affluent two-thirds, by redundancies, occasional tax increases, occasional mortgage interest rate increases and so on – evidence that the capitalist system cannot be trusted – there always seems to be a majority who are quite content to put their trust in the system. They are quite happy, in other words, to remain dependent on the capitalist system. Their reward for this dependence is increasing consumer autonomy.

In recent times, however, there are signs that all is not well amongst the affluent. The experienced need for a meaningful and satisfying life, often expressed in the priority given to self-concerns which are themselves indicative of the need for a fulfilling and satisfying identity, has emerged as a growing problem. Unlike material deprivations, psychic impoverishment cannot be resolved by the kinds of resources peddled by capitalism. Capitalism cannot provide the resources that can best satisfy the need for a meaningful and satisfying life – it cannot provide friendship, love, loyalty, solidarity and so forth. These kinds of things can only be provided by people for themselves. Capitalism trades in money and commodities. The practices of investment, of productivity, of efficiency, of precise calculation of time, of marketing, of distribution and so on, are all irrelevant to what *human* associations are fundamentally about. All attempts by the capitalist system to submit human relations to these practices transform human relations into relations devoid of what is fundamentally human. Human relations that capitalism makes available in commodity form as services, for example, prostitution, social services, and therapy, are existentially irrelevant. Love, for example, cannot be packaged, sold and bought. It cannot be measured in terms of the investment of time. What on earth might it mean to submit love to the practices of productivity and efficiency?

Of course there are trends to commodify human relations, as for example in education, but the increasing commodification of what is essentially non-commodifiable is futile and exacerbates our experience of their meaninglessness. As this trend continues the need for meaning and satisfaction will be more sharply exposed.

Capitalism has reached a stage in its development in which what it provides in quantity for the affluent does not translate into quality. It provides resources for the affluent that are in excess of material need, and denies people the resources that can satisfy the need for a meaningful life. We are thus approaching a time when the dependency of the affluent on the capitalist system will no longer deliver what they most need.

In its relentless pursuit of profit capitalism can move in only one direction, and that is to produce more of what we do not need. Gorz explains:

> To make it worth investing increasing amounts of capital ... it is clearly necessary that increasing production should find purchasers, and therefore that consumption should continue to expand well beyond the satisfaction of actually *felt* needs.[1]

The logic of capitalism is opposed to need satisfaction because there is a limit to the goods required for the satisfaction of survival needs. Only so much food, for example, can be consumed in one day, or in a lifetime come to that. To eat in excess of what we need, both in the short term and in the long term, damages our health and thus our survival. 'Wants and the desire for the superfluous are, by contrast, potentially unlimited.'2 Thus, not only does the meeting of unsatisfied survival needs 'by transferring revenue from the rich to the poor' run 'counter to economic rationality ...', but:

> ... such a transfer would come down to increasing need-determined demand which seeks satisfaction *at the lowest cost*, at the expense of fashion- and fancy-led demand which lends itself to any and every extravagance.
>
> To maintain economic activity it thus makes more sense to provide for the rich rather than the poor ... and, as a result, to innovate continuously in 'top of the range' products, with considerable symbolic value, rather than in the area of products bought for their use value.3

So there is a growing discrepancy between experienced need and the economic activity of capitalism. Capitalism is not interested in producing the goods most needed by those struggling to survive, and it is incapable of providing the conditions in which a meaningful and satisfying life can be lived. In fact the capitalist system, through its colonisation of the life-world (see pp. 21–3), continues to destroy the conditions which constitute the material and social infrastructure that enables the majority of people to live meaningful lives. A major task for emancipatory politics is to create new social conditions to enable people to avoid meaninglessness and to improve the quality of their lives. This, I shall argue later, involves nothing less than the development of a particular kind of culture – a culture of opposition.

Such a major undertaking, while involving initiatives from the politically committed in the early stages, cannot get very far without the involvement of increasing numbers of people. Culture, in its truest sense, is something people live and make for themselves. People cannot make their own culture unless they are resourced to do so. Currently, as we have seen, the affluent are over-provided with resources that are irrelevant to experienced needs, and under-provided with resources relevant to meaningful autonomy. Somehow in order to expand their sphere of autonomy people need to be resourced for autonomy. Consistent with the manipulation of needs thesis, and closely following the kind of thinking best represented by Gorz, I shall argue that resourcing people for autonomy involves, above all else, seizing our time. More than this, Gorz's politics of time is the best bet we have not only for expanding the sphere of autonomy and thus breaking out of our dependency on capitalism, but also for ensuring that in a world of plenty nobody need suffer from a deprivation of their survival needs. The politics of time, I am claiming, should be the practical focus of oppositional politics. It is the lever that can facilitate the development of a culture of opposition.

The Politics of Time

For those in employment, and for many of those who are dependent for their survival on an employed person, life is largely controlled by the demands of employment. Employment involves the performance of 'heteronomous' tasks, that is work, which 'whatever level of skill is required, its form and content are determined by technical imperatives independent of all individual choice and interpretation; these imperatives severely limit the scope for individual judgement and initiative'.[4] To the extent that employment structures our time, and thus in the long term structures our lives, it can be said that our lives, both in employment and in our 'free time', are heterodetermined. Our need to survive, given current arrangements in the advanced capitalist societies, necessarily involves us in submitting ourselves to the control of others.

The central purpose of the politics of time is to

shrink the sphere of heteronomy to its barest minimum – the efficient production of the necessary – in order to enable the maximum expansion of the sphere of autonomy. As we have seen the need to expand the sphere of autonomy has emerged more sharply in recent times as the experience of meaninglessness and identity crises spreads. Employment is increasingly less able to meet our need for meaning, yet it remains our dominant activity in spite of it being split off from all those activities and forms of life that are experienced as meaningful. Attempts to make work in employment more meaningful, without an expansion of the sphere of autonomy outside of employment, may be of some value for some individuals. 'Humanising work', by involving workers in decisions about company logos, in making suggestions about work conditions, or in planning for ever more efficient production, and so on, is an attempt to get workers to identify more closely with their employers, and to involve themselves more totally and fully in what is essentially heterodetermined, futile and meaningless. Such moves may be experienced as even more alienating than imposed work routines in which there is no pretence that the work is nothing more than the sale of body and time.

The only way in which a meaningful and satisfying life can be made possible is by expanding the sphere of autonomy outside of employment. And the only way that this can happen is by reducing our time in employment. This is not only necessary, but, Gorz argues, possible. It has been made possible by automation.

Technological revolutions in the workplace have reduced the total demand for labour without reducing the volume of goods produced. In fact more and more goods are being produced with decreasing amounts of labour. As a consequence the advanced capitalist societies are witnessing their highest ever recorded levels of unemployment. We know that a certain level of unemployment is beneficial to the capitalist system, but it is hardly beneficial to individuals. Do we sit back and allow the capitalist system to dispense with workers 'here' and 'there', and submit ourselves to the insecurities this provokes? Or, do we take matters into our own hands? We have a choice. 'The choice is: *either* a socially controlled, emancipatory abolition of work *or* its oppressive, anti-social abolition.'[5]

The 'anti-social abolition' of work will continue to be a feature of life in the advanced capitalist societies unless we intervene. We can intervene in one of two ways. In order to prevent redundancies we can attempt to reach agreements with employers, as workers are currently doing in France and Germany, which share out the total volume of work among all employees.[6] This strategy is essentially one of survival, affecting workers in 'this' company or 'that' company. In spite of its limitations it nevertheless indicates the willingness of workers to work less and earn less. Alternatively, and this is where a society-wide emancipatory politics is required, we can develop a *social policy* that affects everyone by distributing the total labour requirements of the whole society among all the employable. Gorz is emphatic that the 'emancipatory abolition' of work must involve the development of a 'coherent general *policy*. The point is not to redistribute existing jobs and resources but to *manage an ongoing dynamic process which demands less and less work but creates more and more wealth.*'[7]

The management of savings in labour time in order to allow everybody to work and to work less obviously follows 'principles not of economic rationality but of justice'.[8] More than this, such management, within a general policy, will allow the realm of economics to be subordinated to needs. Thus in addition to the savings in labour time that are made possible by automation, further reductions of quite significant proportions can be made. Thus Gorz argues that:

> there is a rapid decline in the amount of labour-time necessary to reproduce not *this* society ... but a viable society endowed with everything useful and necessary to life ... The amount of time spent working and the relatively high level of employment have been artificially maintained because of the inextricable confusion which exists between the production

of the necessary and the superfluous, the useful and the useless, waste and wealth, pleasures and nuisances, destruction and repair.[9]

Under capitalism the production of the necessary, as we have seen, gets progressively subordinated to the production of the superfluous, and consumption gets increasingly divorced from experienced needs. This, Gorz argues:

> would have been much more difficult *if individuals had been free to adjust their hours of work to the income which they felt they needed.* As productivity and real wages rose during a period of growth, an increasing proportion of the population would have chosen to work less. But workers were never allowed to adjust the hours they put in to the amount of money they felt would take care of their needs.[10]

Shortly, following Gorz, I shall indicate how significant reductions in labour time can be achieved. If working hours were reduced substantially people would have more time to do more for themselves and each other. This would reduce the demand for all sorts of services and goods that people currently buy because of a lack of time. As a consequence further reductions in heterodetermined labour time can be envisaged, personal and family expenditure can be reduced, and the amount of income needed correspondingly reduced. Further, all these reductions not only diminish our dependency on the sphere of heteronomy but do so in ways that improve the quality of life for everyone. This point can be illustrated by reference to the experience of many young parents, and particularly single mothers. If single mothers want to avoid the sub-survival existence provided by welfare benefits, for themselves and their children, they *must* work. As things currently stand the survival prospects of members of the family are dependent on income, the level of which is heterodetermined, as too are the hours to be worked and their scheduling. As a result single mothers are obliged to work to survive *and* to pay for the child-minding services they *have to use* because they are at work. The work is invariably low paid and meaningless, and leaves mothers with very little time and energy for their children. Meanwhile the children are denied the benefit of mothers' caring, experiencing instead a substitute caring, one that is often inappropriately commodified and institutionalised. What we have here is an example of the expansion of the realm of heterodetermined necessity – it has expanded to include the necessary purchase of a service that most mothers would normally prefer to take care of themselves, and that mothers could provide much better. Generally the heterodetermined work available to young, single mothers could be performed by anyone, but there is no adequate substitute for parental love. The reproduction of the impoverishment of young, single mothers and their children is virtually guaranteed while the satisfaction of survival needs is heterodetermined.

The politics of time, as developed by Gorz, would abolish this kind of madness. Gorz estimates that at the beginning of the twenty-first century, given the current declining rate of labour required in the advanced capitalist economies, it will be possible to reduce the working year from the 1,600 hours that it is at present to 1,000 hours. Working requirements over a lifetime could thus be reduced from the current 40,000 – 50,000 to 20,000 – 30,000 hours. These estimates assume that *all* those who are employable work, and this presupposes that everybody has the right to work. It is this right that will be materialised in the form of a guaranteed income. Further, Gorz maintains that a 'decrease in working hours must not entail a decrease in real income, since more wealth is being created by less labour'.[11] The guaranteed income 'will make purchasing power dependent *not on the amount of working hours put in but on the amount of social wealth produced*'.[12]

Gorz considers a number of practical ways of realising a *'policy* of reducing working time' which 'will have as its objective to allow the whole population to benefit from the increase in wealth created and in the savings in working time achieved throughout society as a whole'.[13] Whatever the method of funding the guaranteed income, the important principle is that '*Income should not become independent of work itself, but of working time.*'[14] It is the enactment of this principle in social planning that will enable not only staged reductions in working time for everyone, but also the possibility of the self-management of time and life by individuals. Our obligation to work, implied in the guaranteed income, can be fulfilled at times and periods in our lives when it most suits. Working time does not have to be continuous – it can be intermittent in any number of ways.[15] The problems that currently afflict single mothers need not exit. More than this, the politics of time offers practical emancipation for everyone. Of course not everyone will see it like this. The capitalist class and their favoured subordinates, who between them are virtually the sole beneficiaries of savings in labour time and increasing wealth, will not want to lose their wealth or power. They will do all they can to prevent the development of a *policy* that is likely to lead to people choosing to consume less. They will use all of their power to prevent the expansion of meaningful autonomy for everyone.

If we want an expansion of meaningful autonomy *we will have to make it happen, and this will involve conflict with the capitalist system.* The arguments that I have presented throughout much of this book indicate that *we are already in conflict with the capitalist system,* but as yet this conflict is privatised. Why endure this conflict in isolation? The time has surely come to collectivise the conflict and to make it oppositional to the capitalist system. What might this mean?

A Culture for Autonomy

Clearly an expansion of meaningful autonomy can come about only through an effective oppositional politics. As I noted in the Introduction, the potential support for various social movements is vast, but only a small proportion of this support is activated in sustained participation. If an oppositional movement is to be effective it must organise and conduct itself in ways that attract and sustain participation. And, I shall argue, this involves conducting politics in ways that are not normally considered to be 'political'. More specifically I shall maintain that participation is more likely to be forthcoming if an oppositional movement adopts practices that are supportive of identity needs. The movement, in addition to its focus on issues which define its particular concerns, for example, ecological, patriarchal, and so on, should address the identity needs of its own members in order to make participation attractive and meaningful. A flourishing, dynamic movement not only addresses issues of moral concern but also creates an environment that enables participation as a way of life. We can begin to see what this might mean by identifying practices that deter rather than attract participation.

Oppositional politics is typically concerned with the practical expression of ideological commitments, through demonstrations, marches, newspapers, pamphlets, speeches and so on. In a sense the underlying concern is to prepare the ideological ground of political opposition. Oppositional politics, in this approach, cannot really happen until people have been won over ideologically, hence the emphasis on ideological struggle. In this conception there is an important role for 'culture', not culture as a way of life, but culture as something associated with the arts, whether 'highbrow' or popular. Cultural products, such as pop concerts, comedy shows, films, plays and so forth, that contain content which might be deemed to be oppositional to the dominant ideology, are viewed as potentially influential on the consciousness of individuals, and thus as contributing to the ideological struggle.

There is obviously a need to contest continuously the dominant ideology, to criticise the workings of the capitalist system, to expose the role of the capitalist state in maintaining patriarchy and racism, to criticise the hypocrisy of governments when their actions contradict their official policies, and so forth. But if the ideological struggle is to have the desired impact then it must be conducted in ways that are relevant to people's experienced needs. This presupposes a knowledge of what these needs are, which in turn means that we develop a sensitivity to people's experience, we let them speak for themselves and listen to what they have to say. Too much of what goes on in the name of ideological struggle is patronising, telling people what they already know, insulting of their intelligence, and thoroughly insensitive to their experience.

Far from gaining support, let alone political participation, ideological struggle, when conducted as a process of enlightening the masses, can have opposite effects. For, implicit in such a process are social relations that have no place in a participatory ethos, and thus no place in the conduct of oppositional politics. In short there is no place for relations in which the politically committed assume authority over others. Such relations are essentially inegalitarian, reproduce features of relations of domination and subordination, promote what Paulo Freire refers to as 'anti-dialogical communication',[16] and more or less guarantee the continuing alienation of the ordinary person from organised politics.

With some exceptions, most notably elements of the women's movement, oppositional politics has been conducted in ways that reproduce the dominance of a politically committed elite. The elite 'pull the strings', the rank and file are expected to comply, and the by-standing public are treated as a mass to be addressed in the hope that they might support a political programme designed by the elite. Social relations within elite-led political organisations are subordinated to instrumental goals and serve the maintenance of the organisation. The organisations tend to take on the characteristics of *any* organisation, including business and military, in which people are fitted to the functional requirements of hierarchically ordered positions. As a consequence people tend to relate to each other through roles pertaining to their respective positions, and not as autonomous beings. There is little wonder that the human being who might venture into the political organisation finds himself or herself in alien territory.

In all political organisations of the Left there are too few people doing too many of the important tasks, and too many people confined to non-activity, or to a limited range of menial tasks. A more equal and sensible division of labour is not possible within organisations dominated by the authority of an elite. As a consequence there is a wastage of talents and competencies among the rank and file, an under-participation, and the generation of incompetence at the top (which permeates the whole organisation) arising from a few trying to do too much. Rank and file members are confined to the same kind of lowly status shared by all subordinate groups. They are expected to leaflet, to drive reluctant voters to polling stations, to sell raffle tickets, newspapers and jumble, collect subscriptions, take minutes at meetings mortified by committee procedure, freeze on demonstrations, march for miles in unpredictable weather, form part of a crowd in the middle of a field to hear the important ones deliver worn out speeches, and so on. These kinds of tasks draw on mundane clerical skills, the ownership of waterproof clothing, the ownership of private transport, energy and time that might be more meaningfully used, and the willingness to be one of a herd.

Needless to say any oppositional politics that seeks to expand its participatory base cannot be served by such a model. Active participation implies the exercise of autonomy. Consequently oppositional politics must be organised and conducted in ways that facilitate rather than impede the exercise of autonomy. Consistent with the arguments of the two previous chapters, practices that are most likely to facilitate the exercise and development of autonomy are those that fuel the satisfaction of identity needs. But it is misleading to talk of 'practices' as if there is a blueprint detailing what needs to be done. Rather what needs to be developed in oppositional politics is a culture driven and permeated by genuine *human concern*. Such a culture, a culture for autonomy, is indispensable for sustaining active participation in contestatory politics, and thus for the development of an oppositional culture.

The distinctive feature of a culture of opposition is that it is rooted in human relations that are relations among autonomous beings. In a culture of opposition relations of domination and subordination, of autonomy and dependence, are abolished. Human relations within a culture of opposition must be equal rather than unequal, warm and personal rather than cold and impersonal, stable and enduring rather than unstable and transient, mutually respectful rather than disrespectful, liberating rather than constraining. What we are after is a quality of human relationships that ensures not only ideal conditions for the practical expansion of collective autonomy, but conditions that individuals will find irresistible.

The attractiveness of oppositional politics cannot depend solely on its moral appeal, or in the case of a politics of time, its existential appeal of having more time to exercise more control over one's life. It must also make participation itself attractive (rather than a chore), and this is why we must give priority to relating to each other in mutually supportive ways.

There is however another very important, and timely, reason for transforming the quality of our relationships. I have consistently argued that changes generated by the capitalist system have produced crises centred on the growing experience of meaninglessness, and the increasing difficulties individuals experience in achieving and maintaining a satisfying identity. Identity needs are being exposed. More and more people are seeking help. What help there is – typically in some form of therapy – is quite unsatisfactory. The absence of a satisfactory response to frustrated identity needs suggests a social and cultural failure, but it also indicates that there is a social space for cultural development. Herein lies a real opportunity for emancipatory social movements. Oppositional movements, by helping to develop a culture for autonomy, can make a massive difference to people's lives. Through developing and establishing convivial human relationships in all that it does, an oppositional politics can address identity needs. We can begin to do this now. It does not take money, just a little time and a commitment to translate our abstract concern for humanity into a practical concern for the real individuals whom we encounter.

I have argued that there are two basic universal identity needs: ontological security, and a sense of significance. Of the latter Laing maintains that:

> Every human being, whether child or adult, seems to require *significance*, that is, *place in another person's world*. Adults and children seek 'position' in the eyes of others, a position that offers room to move. It is difficult to imagine many who would choose unlimited freedom within a nexus of personal relations, if anything they did had no significance for anyone else.[17]

What I am advocating is that the experience of involvement in oppositional politics should be such that the individual feels important, that he or she feels significant in some way. Obviously we cannot 'fix' another's experience. We can, however, treat the other in certain ways that are more likely to facilitate than block the experience of a sense of significance. We can, for example, do things to involve the other, and to demonstrate that we respect and value their autonomy; we can show an interest in them by asking them about themselves and finding out what their interests are; we can listen to them and ask for their opinion on matters that seem important to them; we can treat them as persons with something to offer; and we can encourage them to express themselves by being self-disclosing, rather than defensive, ourselves.

There is nothing particularly special about these little things that we can do. They are the kinds of thing that do happen in the better human relationships. They certainly do not need to be taught as 'human relations skills' or 'communication skills'. In fact they cannot be taught. They are not skills. They are the kinds of action that flow from a sincere and genuine human concern. Sincerity and human concern cannot be taught, they come from within the person. What does get taught as communication or human relations skills are functions that belong to the machinery of bureaucratic organisations – functions that can be performed by anyone who subordinates their being to instrumental, non-human goals.

Addressing the need for ontological security is far more difficult. Some believe that unless ontological security is established in childhood, insecurity will plague individuals throughout their lives.[18] As a consequence of 'normal' socialisation, Logan has argued, women are more likely than men to experience insecurity as a recurring feature of their lives.[19] It may well be the case that the continuing experience of being loved is most likely to facilitate ontological security. Obviously an oppositional politics cannot be expected to enable such experience. It can, however, do a number of things that might prevent insecurities developing into hopelessness and despair. It is particularly important in this respect to treat others in ways that might facilitate their self-acceptance. This is easier said than done. It does seem to require that we accept others for what they are, that we are non-judgmental of them as persons, in short, that we treat them with what Carl Rogers describes as 'unconditional positive regard'.[20]

In the longer term an oppositional politics has much more to offer. This is where the development of an oppositional culture is so important. An individual's need for ontological security can be met, in part at least, by being embedded in enduring relationships with others on whom he or she can rely and depend on for support when necessary. In other words the experience of ontological security is largely dependent on our being able to invest our trust in others. A culture of opposition, I have already noted, is based on stable, enduring, reciprocal relations of mutual trust. In practice this means that we are honest with each other, we do not betray confidences, we avoid talking behind each other's backs, and that we do not let each other down.

The politically committed have a responsibility to begin to live their politics in the kinds of ways I have suggested if a culture of opposition is to *develop* into a distinct way of life. It is in these ways that a culture of opposition can provide some security for people, some form of community in which identities can be meaningfully confirmed, and the bonds of solidarity necessary for sustaining struggles against the capitalist system.

A Way Forward

All movements seeking emancipatory social change can benefit by beginning to develop a culture for autonomy. All movements, too, can benefit from an expansion of the sphere of autonomy through a reduction in working hours. From the evidence of recent industrial disputes, of recent media attention to unemployment and changing patterns of employment, as well as from the evidence of everyday conversations, it is safe to say that there is a growing sensitivity to issues around working hours. More and more people are questionning the necessity of long working days and weeks, and its contribution to stress. More importantly, there is a growing recognition that it makes little sense to have a situation in which an increasing proportion of those in employment are working longer hours while levels of unemployment remain high. There is thus some foundation to the belief that there would be considerable support for a campaign to develop a social policy of time along the lines advocated by Gorz.

What Gorz has in mind, however, does involve much more than campaigning for a reduction in working hours. As I argued in Chapter 3, working shorter hours, on its own, does not automatically expand the sphere of autonomy. Resources other than time, to use in free time, are necessary for the expansion of autonomy. Without other resources, free time, as the experience of many unemployed people testifies, will be 'empty time', as Gorz describes it. So, for Gorz, a politics of time, in addition to its focus on reducing working hours, must also involve:

1. A politics of collective facilities, which can provide cities, towns and even apartment blocks with places for communication, interchange and autonomous activity ...
2. A politics of voluntary co-operation and association allowing the development of all kinds of local, non-market, collective services, which are more effective, more appropriate and more adaptable, as well as being less expensive, when they are not state-run institutions ... [21]

Gorz provides a number of existing examples of the kind of collective facility that is useful for autonomous activity. He mentions community centres containing facilities for recreation, reading, discussion, adult education, workshops and refreshment. He notes that similar facilities, in addition to communal kitchens and laundries, are available in some apartment blocks in Scandinavia. With respect to autonomous forms of co-operation Gorz refers to an existing range of workers' co-operatives, skills exchanges, self-help groups, transport sharing, child-care co-ops and so on. Additionally there are isolated examples of de-schooling networks in which groups of parents and children plan and enact an education outside of formal schooling, co-operative shops and banks, and experiments in the development of small self-sustaining communities. And, in recent times, in spite of meagre facilities, many unemployment centres have spawned a wide range of voluntary community services.

Of course these kinds of activities will not appeal to everyone, perhaps not even to a majority. But that is not the point. All kinds of things are possible given the facilities and the time. What is important is that the politics of time must proceed hand-in-hand with a politics of collective facilities and with a politics of voluntary co-operation if the practical expansion of meaningful autonomy for everyone is to be realised. If these politics are successful more and more people will experience the benefits and satisfactions that ensue from activities and projects that they plan, organise and manage for themselves. It can be supposed that the experienced satisfactions will fuel the need for the continuing expansion of the sphere of autonomy. In a sense, beyond a certain level of success, these politics will become self-propelling, and those involved will be moving toward constructing for themselves a way of life that reduces their dependency on the capitalist system.

It is one thing to speculate about a possible (some would say 'unlikely') future, and quite another to spell out how it can come about. In truth there is no easy way forward. Very few people have the time or inclination to involve themselves in what they anticipate will be a long, drawn-out, struggle for little practical gain. Gorz, himself, 'appeals' to the labour movement. He directs his proposals to trade unionists and 'other left activists'. The labour movement is, after all, the best organised and best resourced of all the potential opposition to the capitalist system. For Gorz, this 'confers on it a particular responsibility'.[22] He argues that:

> The labour movement should not forget ... that its origins lie in working-class cultural associations. It will not be able to survive as a movement unless it takes an interest in people's self-realization outside their work as well as in it, and helps or participates in the creation of sites and spaces in which people are able to develop their ability to take responsibility for their own lives and self-manage their social relations ... [23]

Many trade unionists are recognising that the future of unions is not a particularly rosy one if current trends continue. Unions are losing members as more and more companies seek contractual arrangements with individual employees in order to subvert collective bargaining, and prefer to hire part-time, temporary labour. Unions are getting smaller, and in the context of high levels of unemployment they are losing their bargaining power. Gorz is surely correct to suggest that the survival of unions is dependent on them taking 'an interest in people's self-realization outside their work as well as in it'. Just as important is the need for unions to broaden their concerns beyond those of protecting the interests of their own members.

Unions already possess, in populous localities, the facilities that could be used for autonomous forms of co-operation and association. And the labour movement as a whole is the only movement well placed to launch a vigorous politics of time. But an emancipatory politics of time implies the development of a social policy that affects everyone – the employed *and* unemployed, union members *and* non-members. The hope is that unions will arrest their decline by opening themselves up to the public, and deploying their resources to enable an expansion of the sphere of autonomy. This is just the kind of boost that is necessary for a culture for autonomy to develop.

A culture for autonomy in its early stages can thus develop without contestation against the capitalist system. At the same time, however, it provides a basis for future contestation. The experience of combining one's own efforts with others, of group planning, of co-operation, of mutual support and so forth, develops the kind of solidarity required for engaging in forms of collective contestation against the capitalist system. It is impossible to imagine a *continuing* expansion of the sphere of autonomy without contestation over time, resources and facilities. The resources of the trade unions, while essential in the early stages of cultural development, are insufficient to accommodate a continuously expanding sphere of autonomy.

From our present position the prospect of having to contest the power of the capitalist system would seem to render any politics headed in that direction totally unfeasible. But from a future position, in which vast numbers of people have developed a culture for autonomy for themselves, the prospect of having to engage in conflict with the capitalist system is far less daunting. Having already experienced the value of collective self-determination, people will be more prepared to engage in contestation, and will be more hopeful that collective action will yield success.

6 Conclusion:
On a Culture of Opposition

The main ideas that have led me to propose the need for a culture of opposition can be enumerated as follows:

1. The scale, pace and intensity of social changes in the advanced capitalist societies over the past 30 years or so have had a profound effect on people's lived experience. Against the views that celebrate these changes as heralding new freedoms for the individual, I have emphasised that life in the advanced capitalist societies is such that an increasing number of people are experiencing difficulties in achieving a meaningful and satisfying life. For some these difficulties result in identity crisis.

2. In spite of all the changes that are transforming the social context in which we live, relations of domination and subordination continue to persist as enduring characteristics of the advanced capitalist societies. Of these relations, which include class, sex and race relations, that between the capitalist system and the vast majority affects everybody's life, and has thus been the focus of my concerns.

3. There has been a tendency to explain the continuing presence of relations of domination and subordination in terms of ideological manipulation – that is, the belief that the subordinate are kept in a state of subordination primarily by the effects of dominant ideologies. In recent times such a view has been heavily criticised and is falling from favour. Nevertheless it is still widely assumed that our actions are largely controlled by what is inside our heads. This assumption is part and parcel of what I have called 'ideology-centred' thinking.

Ideology-centred thinking, and with it a psycho-centric view of individuals, remains influential in explaining both the reproduction of relations of domination and subordination, and the responses of individuals to these changing times.

4. In opposition to ideology-centred thinking, I have emphasised that ideological motivations are of little importance in the lives of the subordinate, and are essentially irrelevant in explaining their actions. Of far greater importance are needs-based motivations.

5. I have argued that in addition to the need to survive we all have a need for a meaningful and satisfying life, and that this need translates into a need for autonomy.

6. Both the reproduction of relations of domination and subordination, and the experience of meaninglessness and identity crisis can be best understood in terms of how the capitalist system maintains the vast majority in dependence on it, and how this results in declining opportunities for the exercise of meaningful autonomy.

7. In order to survive people are, directly or indirectly, dependent on employment or welfare. Those dependent on welfare are insufficiently resourced for a meaningful use of time. Those dependent on employment, most of which is experienced as meaningless, are deprived of time and energy for meaningful autonomy. Either way autonomy is restricted and under-developed. By controlling the resources that enable individuals to act, the capitalist system determines the range of action available to individuals.

8. The pursuit of profit ensures that production is geared to over-supplying the affluent with goods that are irrelevant to their needs, and it necessarily involves confining the vast majority globally, and a substantial minority within the advanced capitalist

societies, to poverty. The capitalist system is thus out of sync with what people need.

9. Capitalism supplies a majority within the advanced capitalist societies with resources that promote private consumption. Increasing numbers of people are experiencing consumer-based lifestyles as inadequate in meeting the need for a meaningful and satisfying life. With opportunities for meaningful autonomy restricted, the vast majority seek satisfactions and meaning in the private sphere. The resource limitations of the private sphere make this search, for some, precarious. As a consequence issues central to self-identity loom large in the lives of a growing number of people. Self-preoccupations centred on 'coping' on the one hand, or 'self-actualisation' on the other, form part of the dominant cultural trend, privatism.

10. Against those views that see contemporary absorptions with self-identity as signalling the freedom to pursue post-necessity lifestyles, I have argued that they are best seem as symptomatic of identity crisis resulting from unmet identity needs.

11. Identities are inherently social, and identity needs can only be met through the actions of others. The development of an autonomous self can provide protection against identity crisis, but this too is dependent on the actions of others. Privatistic responses to identity crisis are essentially unsatisfactory. But in the absence of social support, and socialisation practices that facilitate the development of autonomy, individuals will continue to resort to privatism.

12. All forms of privatism are forms of social withdrawal and political abstinence. It is thus perverse to see in the contemporary preoccupations with self-identity the emergence of a new politics. On the contrary, privatistic lifestyles help to secure the reproduction of the capitalist system.

13. In the absence of an effective opposition to the capitalist system it will continue to wreak havoc with people's lives, and people will become increasingly submerged in privatism.

14. The trend toward privatism and identity crises can be halted and reversed by resourcing people for autonomy. But since essential resources for autonomy are controlled by the capitalist system, resourcing people for autonomy involves contestation with the capitalist system.

15. We are faced with the choice of either continuing to submit our lives to the control of the capitalist system or of breaking out of its grip.

16. Loosening our dependence on the capitalist system involves developing and expanding the sphere of autonomy for the majority. The expansion of the sphere of autonomy thus not only alters our relation to the capitalist system by reducing our dependence on it, it is also the key to the achievement of a meaningful and satisfying life. As such, the expansion of that sphere of autonomy embraces the traditional and more contemporary concerns of emancipatory politics, and is thus an appropriate unifying focus for oppositional politics.

17. The expansion of the sphere of autonomy involves an increase in resourced time for everyone in social conditions conducive to the exercise of individual and collective autonomy. The most appropriate vehicle for bringing about an increase in resourced time is an emancipatory politics of time in conjunction with a politics of collective resources. The social conditions which best facilitate the exercise of autonomy are what I refer to as a culture for autonomy – a culture grounded in relations characterised by genuine concern for the other, equality, mutual trust and co-operation, and involving the

practical enactment of individual and community-based autonomous projects.

18. A culture for autonomy is a way of life that people make for themselves. However, given that at the present time there is nothing in existence that approximates a society-wide culture for autonomy, and given that such a culture is precisely what is needed to address increasingly frustrated identity needs in particular, and the need for a meaningful and satisfying life more generally, I have suggested that emancipatory social movements have a positive role to play in promoting this culture by beginning to enact some of its key features.

19. All emancipatory social movements, by incorporating the need to develop a culture for autonomy, have an opportunity to increase their membership, and sustain political participation.

20. A culture for autonomy and an emancipatory politics of resourced time are mutually reinforcing. Taken together as an integrated whole, they constitute a movement for the expansion of the sphere of autonomy.

21. A culture for autonomy is the foundation for a culture of opposition. A culture for autonomy becomes a culture of opposition as the continuing expansion of the sphere of autonomy increasingly necessitates contestation against the capitalist system. Bonds of solidarity, which develop as a consequence of people's practical involvement with each other on autonomous projects, are vital in sustaining participation in contestatory politics.

No doubt my discussion of a politics for expanding the sphere of autonomy raises many more questions than it answers. I shall attempt to begin to answer a few of the more obvious questions below.

Is not the emphasis on autonomy an expression of the ideology individualism?

It is important to distinguish between two quite distinct approaches to the concept of autonomy. On the one hand autonomy is treated as a property of the individual, and is thus part and parcel of the ideology of individualism. On the other hand, and this is the approach I have adopted, autonomy is viewed, first and foremost, as something that is *enabled* by the resources available to the individual.

Within the ideology of individualism what makes an individual autonomous are natural abilities, for example intelligence, and natural personality characteristics, for example assertiveness. When aligned with the view, commonplace in right-wing 'thought', that these so called natural properties are unevenly distributed among people, and are the natural basis of human differences, we end up with a justification not only for social inequalities but also for their repressive reinforcement. Not that long ago a member of the British Cabinet proclaimed that 'had God intended equality he would not have created men and women'.[1]

For those on the Right it thus follows that women are naturally less autonomous than men, and that it is a waste of their time to struggle against nature. It further follows, within this view, that it makes natural sense for women to accept their subordination to male authority. This obviously leads to a position in which the reproduction of male domination is actually advocated. Thus a co-author of an influential report wrote:

> I believe that in addition to their needs as individuals, girls should be educated in terms of their main social function – which is to make for themselves, their children and their husbands a secure and suitable home, and to be mothers.[2]

It is exactly this kind of thinking that has been, and still is, used to justify class, racial and imperial forms of domination. It was not that long ago when employ-

ers advertised for 'hands' – the distinguishing natural
property of working class people! If autonomy is seen
as a natural property of the individual, and if some
groups are deemed to be better endowed than others,
then what better justification for a social order that
systematically denies the majority the freedom to determine their own existence. In the words of a right-
winger:

> If a society is to prosper, its political, social and
> economic arrangements must be such as to stimulate
> and satisfy those with most to contribute to the
> common good. In any society, at any time, there are
> some citizens who have more to contribute than
> others, and it is in everybody's interest that this
> outstanding minority should exercise more influence
> over public affairs than the untalented minority:
> should form, that is to say, a ruling class ... [3]

Translated to a global scale we can end up with the
questions: 'Why should publicly financed resources (in
the under-developed countries) be devoted to preventing infant mortality when the economic worth of such
marginal infants is negative?' The two scientists who
posed this question went on to state that 'the economy
would be better off without them'.[4] In other words the
natural endowments of some people are so meagre that
they are of little use to society. Needless to say such a
view is a component of racist ideology, and can be
used to justify the denial of human rights, contemporary forms of slavery, and genocide.[5]

I would not suggest for one minute that if we
think that autonomy is a natural property of individuals we must necessarily embrace right-wing ideologies. There is nevertheless a danger of moving in that
direction – not all the way, but certainly as far as
having insufficient faith in people's abilities to be
autonomous. This is the danger inherent in some of
the recent discussions on human rights in which it is
assumed that people living in the advanced capitalist
societies *are* free to exercise what Gorz refers to as

'sovereign control over their own lives and ways of
co-operating with others'.[6] Of course Gorz is stating
this as what should be the case rather than what is
the case. While most people know that the majority
do not have this right, by virtue of being compelled
to be dependent on the capitalist system, and that as
a consequence some freedoms or choices are not
available to them, it is nevertheless commonly
assumed that the choices people make tell us more
about them as individuals than about the restrictions
of their circumstances. And it is this assumption that
is central to the ideology of individualism.

The ideology of individualism embraces the view that
the source of an individual's autonomy resides within
the self, whether in the form of natural, unchanging
properties, or in the form of personality characteristics
or qualities of consciousness. It follows from this view
that the expansion of autonomy is primarily a matter of
'working on' individuals, of changing their personalities
or their consciousness. It further follows that a politics
for autonomy, which is underpinned by the ideology of
individualism, boils down to education and therapy. It
is a politics that leaves social conditions intact, or at
best assumes that society will change as a consequence
of individuals being changed.

In sharp contrast, I have argued that the exercise
of autonomy is dependent more on the resources
external to the individual than on self-resources.
Indeed self-resources are dependent for their development on resources residing outside of the self. We all
have the capacity for autonomy, but the development
and exercise of this capacity is primarily a social
matter. Consequently, in this approach a politics for
autonomy is focused on increasing the availability of
resources relevant for the individual's autonomy.

*Is not such a politics limited in its appeal? Does everybody
experience the need for autonomy?*

I have attempted to establish that there is a widespread
and growing need for the development and exercise of

autonomy, which is not to say that everybody experiences this need as urgent. Rather, people experience lack of time, lack of space, lack of money, meaninglessness, insecurity, a lack of significance, boredom, depression, powerlessness, and so forth. Many of these experiences have an intangible quality. As Kate Soper argues, their intangibility, in comparison with the experienced deprivation of survival needs, makes them 'less obviously felt'. She elaborates:

> If you are deprived of food, you feel the pangs of hunger; if you are deprived of love, or of opportunities for creative activity, or of the space and time that are preconditions of any self-development, you do not so much feel the loss as lose the power to feel – you become the victim of a vicious regress, caught up in a process that numbs sensitivity in the very act of depriving it.[7]

Not only is this true, but prolonged experience of this kind can immobilise people. Soper goes on to argue that:

> psychological deprivation of this kind is felt less urgently the more extensive it becomes, since it is part of the process of deprivation that one loses the power to feel that anything is urgent. In this sense, non-fulfilment of these psychological needs tends to be self-sustaining and self-perpetuating: it breeds not indignation, but apathy, and a sense of futility of any political initiative.[8]

There is an added difficulty. When we experience hunger we recognise a *need* for food. But it has yet to be established in people's minds that we need more autonomy to prevent experiences of meaninglessness and similar deprivations. However, the analysis of meaninglessness and identity crisis suggests that these experiences do have a source in the lack of opportunities that exist for the exercise of meaningful autonomy. We readily recognise that food is a need to prevent and satisfy hunger. In the same way it can be said that autonomy is a *need* to prevent psychological deprivations and to satisfy the quest for a more meaningful existence.

A society which is intent on attempting to remove starvation will develop, and put into practice, an appropriate food policy. If we are to remove meaninglessness and identity crisis, we will need to develop a long term policy for the expansion of the sphere of autonomy. And, among other things, this will mean the development of social conditions – a culture for autonomy – in which identity needs can be best satisfied.

Nevertheless, it is difficult to imagine those with a prolonged experience of a lack of autonomy suddenly becoming autonomous.

First, people do not *suddenly* become autonomous from a position of powerlessness. It takes time. There is no quick 'fix' whereby the most dependent can be transformed into highly autonomous beings. This is why I emphasise that there is a need to *develop* a culture for autonomy.

Secondly, we cannot draw conclusions about individuals' ability to be autonomous that are based on observations of their current lifestyles. Not only do current lifestyles reflect the resources that are available to individuals, *and* resources that are not available, but they also bear the effects of socialisation practices. Individuals are socially produced, so to speak, and they are being socially produced in ways that impede rather than facilitate the development of autonomy. In this respect one can consider the role played by the education system.

As I have argued earlier, schools place priority on teaching for certification. Above all else this involves teaching children to fashion themselves to the requirements of the labour market. Those who are most successful at self-commodification, the exact opposite of being autonomous, get the better jobs. Much that occurs in adult education, too, is patronising and insulting. This is particularly true of the attempts to make the unemployed employable. Here I am thinking of a

variety of practices, ranging from instruction on how to
apply for a job, how to conduct oneself at an interview,
to retraining for jobs that either do not exist or, if they
did, do not require any training at all.

We should not be surprised if many of those who
have suffered a long experience of not being treated as
autonomous display a lack of a sense of self as autonomous. However, this does not mean that they have
totally lost their capacity for autonomy.

*It seems, from your comments on the education system, that
the development of a culture for autonomy requires a
radical transformation of education policy. Is this feasible?*

Not just education policy, but socialisation practices
generally. If a culture for autonomy is to develop and
reproduce itself it must socialise future generations for
autonomy.

Socialisation practices are more or less geared to the
requirements of the society into which the individual is
socialised. This is particularly true of formal education.
In a rapidly changing society it is difficult for established institutionalised socialisation, such as formal
schooling, to adapt to new requirements. In the
advanced capitalist societies policy-makers have recognised that their planning must address a rapidly changing labour market. Thus in recent years schools and
universities have been modifying their curricula to meet
employers' needs for transferable skills and employee
'flexibility'. Even so there is a growing awareness that
there is no longer a neat fit between schooling and
employment.

Many parents already know that their children are
growing up in a society that cannot guarantee future
employment, let alone a meaningful career. Many
teachers already know this too. The time is ripe for
public debate on the role of education. It does not
make sense to continue to pour public money into an
education system which is geared to servicing employers. Most jobs can be performed by anyone, with no
special skills or training, and the more demanding jobs

are best learned on the job itself. Employers themselves have more faith in their own training programmes than anything schools or universities can provide.

This is not to say that employers are ready to consider a radical transformation of the education system. Schooling is valued by employers not so much for its curricular content but more for its 'expertise' in socialising young people for a future of subordination.

Teachers, as much recent media publicity reveals, are becoming increasingly disillusioned with their jobs. They may well be receptive to changes more in keeping with the development of a culture for autonomy. At least many teachers would welcome dispensing with the task of keeping pupils busy on irrelevances – one of the ways in which young people are prepared for subordination. As former teachers Trevor Blackwell and Jeremy Seabrook put it:

> How we longed to pass on something of real value, other than dictated notes on the six causes of the French revolution, or the tragic flaw in Hamlet's character ... We would have liked to share with our pupils the inescapability of suffering and laughter, of fear, desire, mortality and joy, and to have shown how these human experiences are handled in other cultures, as well as our own.[9]

While such sentiments are not unusual among teachers, it must be said that the history of educational reform suggests that the most significant changes to the education system have been instigated by political forces outside of the teaching profession. Besides, even among teachers who might favour change in a more humanistic direction, energies are consumed by either enacting or opposing demands from the state, rather than in seeking an alternative. Yet if we are to develop a culture for autonomy we will need an education system that serves this culture. However, the impetus for the necessary changes in education and other forms of socialisation are more likely to come from a society-wide movement for the expansion of the sphere of autonomy than from initiatives within the teaching profession. This is so because such a movement will have to address the fundamental question: do we bring up and educate children to adapt to, and take their place in, a system that grants them little significant control over their own lives, or do we bring up and educate children to become autonomous?

What would an education for autonomy involve?

My analysis in Chapter 4 (see pp. 88–90) suggests that from an early age young children need to be in an environment in which autonomy is valued, which is peopled by adults who are 'behavioural models' of autonomous persons, and in which they are encouraged to be autonomous by experiencing love and emotional support from the adults on whom they are dependent. As they grow older the development of autonomy will require increasing access to a wide range of skills, and increasing opportunities to exercise autonomy. Individuals will need to be in an environment in which they are free to plan and manage individual and group projects, in which they gain experience in combining their own autonomy with the autonomy of others in co-operative relations, and in which they are encouraged to debate and discuss all those issues relevant to playing an active role in helping to shape the society in which they live.

You seem to be advocating an education pioneered by the 'free school' movement.[10] Yet this movement has had little impact either on the education system, or on society.

The free school movement and other alternatives to state-provided education have arisen out of the efforts of parents who for one reason or another are dissatisfied with the schooling provided by the state, *and* have the time and other resources to provide an alternative education for their children. The impact of this movement will be limited because only a very small minority of people among those critical of existing educational provision have the resources to realistically contemplate an alternative. Additionally, parents tend to remain involved in alternative forms of education only while their children are of an age which legally requires them to attend school.

As for the influence of free schools on the education system, there is little scope in the established system for practices that run counter to its main functions. Gerry Adams correctly observes that:

An educational system which taught people to question their society, their environment, their social or economic disadvantage, an educational system which assisted people to strive for the common good, to form and voice radical opinions, to seek change, would do no service to those in control of the social and economic order ... [11]

Similarly the powers that be are not going to encourage autonomy, except in those limited ways that are readily accommodated within the capitalist system.

The impact of the free school movement has been limited for the reasons I have suggested and, perhaps more importantly, by virtue of its isolation from a broader, society-wide social movement. Nevertheless, the very existence of parent-provided alternatives to schooling suggests that there are people around who are prepared to develop and manage an education for autonomy. This does augur well for a social movement for the expansion of the sphere of autonomy.

You have argued that a movement for autonomy is an appropriate unifying focus for oppositional politics. Why should such a movement prove to be more successful than the existing oppositional movements?

Over 20 years ago Habermas argued that important changes were afoot in the socio-cultural system of the advanced capitalist societies.[12] In an analysis compatible with many of the arguments that I have presented, Habermas suggested that the basis of the legitimation of the capitalist system was being eroded. Legitimation

had been secured, he reasoned, in the capitalist system's ability to meet needs which were embodied in
privatistic syndromes of motivation. Two complemen-
tary forms of privatism, what he referred to as 'civil'
privatism and 'familial-vocational' privatism, had
secured the reproduction of the capitalist system.
Essentially individuals had left 'political' matters to the
politicians (civil privatism) while they got on with their
own careers and with improving their family lives
through consumption and leisure (familial-vocational
privatism). But, as a consequence of the emergence of
a number of crisis tendencies, for example ecological
crisis, which have their source in advanced capitalist
growth, the capitalist system was being placed under
increasing strain. As a result the capitalist system was
no longer able to satisfy the needs of a growing proportion of people. The established patterns of privatism
were being undermined along with the ideologies supporting them. Habermas noted that '"meaning" is a
scarce resource and is becoming ever scarcer'.[13] Not
surprisingly increasing numbers of people were vulnerable to the experience of identity crisis.

Habermas argued that two contradictory outcomes
of identity crisis could be expected: 'withdrawal as a
reaction to an overloading of personality resources', and
'protest as a result of an autonomous ego organization
that cannot be stabilized under the given conditions'.[14]
The former of these possible outcomes, I have argued,
has been the dominant response, resulting in heightened forms of self-absorption.

Protest, over the past 20 years, has been sporadic,
and has not developed into a unified opposition. What
opposition there is tends to be heavily fragmented.

Habermas was not alone in placing hope for progressive social change on the protest potentials embodied in
the new social movement. They do, after all, reflect a
morality that is radically opposed to specific elements of
the capitalist system. The peace movement stands
opposed to the futility of the production of weapons of
destruction and technologies of death; the green movement is opposed to the value of economic growth; and

the women's movement is, among other things, opposed
to male domination, which directly and indirectly has its
basis in the authority wielded by the capitalist state.
There is no doubt, too, that oppositional consciousness is
more widespread today than 20 years ago. There is far
more awareness of racism, of sexism, of the need to
maintain ecological balance, of US imperialism, of state
repression, of capitalism's role in creating and sustaining
poverty in the Third World, and so on.

The new social movements, with one or two small
and isolated exceptions, have not moved beyond ideological struggle. Their radical values have not produced
a new way of life, a new *culture*. They may have
precipitated a reordering of priorities within private
lives but not beyond in the socio-cultural sphere. In a
sense, protest potentials have been privatised, and thus
rendered ineffective. And ironically the spread of radical consciousness also embraces the awareness of the
impotence of the new social movements in the face of
the capitalist system, which reinforces the individual's
own sense of powerlessness. The major difference
between the radical consciousness of the 1960s and
that of today is that today it incorporates a heightened
sense of one's own powerlessness.

In spite of all that is written about the potential of
the existing social movements for bringing about radical
social change there is little evidence of any *movement*.
Major political parties would seem to have given up
any sense of political leadership, confining themselves
to 'crisis management'. The small radical parties are
totally ineffective in making any impact beyond their
own tiny circles. In sum, on the political front there is
little that is going on that grabs the hearts and minds
of the vast majority. Emancipatory politics would seem
to be in decline.

Yet the capitalist system is not providing what most
people need. Furthermore, it is incapable of providing
the kinds of satisfactions that are the basis of a meaningful and satisfying life. We can only provide these
satisfactions for ourselves. People are trying to do just
this privatistically. But privatistic lifestyles are limited

in the satisfactions they can deliver. At best they provide the compensatory satisfactions of consumption,
and at worst destructive forms of self-absorption.

Capitalism's failure, and the failure of privatism, to
meet the need for a meaningful and satisfying life
suggests that there is a cultural vacuum. Somehow this
vacuum needs to be filled with a vibrant culture that is
capable of meeting people's needs. I have argued that
this involves resourcing people for autonomy, hence the
need for a movement intent on expanding the sphere of
autonomy.

The chances of such a movement being successful are
helped by its relevance to the experienced needs of a
growing number of people. Additionally, while like other
social movements a movement for autonomy involves
ideological campaigns, it must also involve the development of conditions in which people are better able to
meet their needs. It thus involves needs-relevant practical activities which, I have maintained, are necessary in
the establishment of an attractive participatory ethos.

*Will not the pursuit of autonomy fragment rather than
unify opposition to the capitalist system?*

If we think of autonomy in terms of individuals doing
their own thing in a context in which people are in
competition with each other for scarce resources it is
difficult to imagine any outcome other than social fragmentation. In a capitalist society this view predominates
because it reflects social reality. It is commonly said, for
example, that your gain is my loss, your privilege is my
disadvantage, and so on. In this context individuals can
only maximise their freedom (autonomy) at the expense
of others. We end up with a 'society' based on the
principle of the survival of the fittest.

The logic of the survival of the fittest applies not
only to individuals. In capitalist societies it can also
apply to groups competing with each other for scarce
resources. The experience of group competition has
been a common one in local politics. Feminists, gays
and ethnic minorities have competed against each

other, and against other organised groups, for limited resources. This has not only fuelled divisions between groups, it has also created resentment among local populations who may feel that the perceived self-indulgences of gays, for example, are being financed at their, the tax-payers' expense.

This kind of scenario will persist unless we come to our senses. The capitalist system controls most of the resources individuals and groups need to expand their autonomy. Instead of competing with each other for the limited resources made available by the capitalist system, why not fight the system? We cannot conduct a successful fight either as isolated individuals or as isolated groups. We have to join forces with each other in order to make more resources available to everyone. This does not mean that groups, such as the women's movement or Greens, give up their particular struggles. It does mean, however, that oppositional groups should avoid competing with each other and seek ways of combining with each other. A movement for expanding the sphere of autonomy would provide an excellent opportunity for oppositional groups to combine on a common interest.

You also seem to be suggesting that we bury our ideological differences. Does this imply that we give up our ideological commitments?

I have noted that interest in the issues raised by various social movements is considerably greater than levels of participation in the movements' activities. Somehow this interest needs to be translated into participation, and sustained participation at that. If we address this problem from what I term 'ideology-centred' thinking, we tend to blame lack of participation on a lack of ideological commitment. This has led many activists into attempting to 'win over' support by ideological argument. In a number of instances this strategy has been successful in influencing public opinion. One has only to think of the ideological gains made by the peace movement, the Greens, and the woman's movement over the past 20 years or so. Yet these gains have

not led to widespread participation. Among those who
have attempted to get involved in some form of political activity very few maintain their involvement. Recognition of this fact has prompted me to argue that we
need to give serious attention to the way in which we
conduct oppositional politics. In this respect an initial
task for all oppositional movements is to rid themselves
of practices that deter participation and begin to adopt
practices that facilitate wider involvement.

For those caught up in ideology-centred thinking this
may sound like I am advocating a deradicalisation of the
demands made by oppositional movements. This, after
all, has been the tendency among left-leaning social
democratic parties in their efforts to gain electoral support. In fact I am advocating something entirely different.
The key to facilitating participation resides in making
involvement in oppositional politics relevant to the needs
of the participants. I have given some indication that this
involves democratising and humanising social relations
within oppositional movements. Translating this into
practice will mean broadening our concept of politics to
incorporate an orientation toward the development of
mutual support among activists.

This does not mean that oppositional movements
should transform themselves into social clubs devoted
to the enjoyment of their own members. But it does
mean that *in addition to* its campaigning role an
oppositional movement, if it is to flourish, must
involve itself with the kind of orientation implicit in
the practical development of a culture for autonomy.
Quite simply, oppositional movements will not be the
force they could be unless they make participation
attractive.

There are numerous examples in everyday life of
people co-operating with each other, and being mutually supportive, even though a wide ideological gulf
may exist between them. What I have proposed does
not involve activists giving up their ideological commitments. Rather, ideological commitments should not
get in the way of needs-relevant activities and
relations.

You suggest that a social movement for the expansion of the sphere of autonomy can be initiated by trade unions. Are not trade unions limited in their appeal?

I have already noted that trade unions are associated with what many perceive to be an outdated politics. They tend not to be attractive organisations, either for their own members or for the general public. On the Left they have been criticised as preserves of male and white privilege, and for pursuing policies – essentially the protection of the narrow interests of their own members – that reproduce ecological imbalance, that contradict the aims of the peace movement, and that sustain the impoverishment of the Third World. In most western societies the oppositional credentials of the trade union movement have been further compromised by the conservatism of many of its leaders, and by its association with rightward-drifting social democratic and labour parties.

I have noted, too, that many trade unionists are aware of these difficulties, and recognise that unions must change if they are to hang on to their members, let alone if they are to have a future influence. Unions are in crisis. But we cannot dismiss out of hand the possibility of unions emerging out of crisis as organisations prepared to take a more proactive role in meeting the needs of members *and* non-members. Indeed, I would maintain that unions will continue to decline unless they make their resources and facilities available to members and non-members alike, in the communities in which they are located, unless they encourage the development of a culture for autonomy, and unless they campaign for an emancipatory politics of time.

Some people are sufficiently resourced either in the private sphere or as part of a wider social network to experience a meaningful and satisfying life. They are, however, a minority. The majority do require resourcing. The unions have an opportunity to make a difference to the lives of those who are insufficiently resourced. Unions are in a position to 'kick-start' a culture for autonomy. In other words, unions are well placed to take initiatives that will enable people to have time and space to generate social practices constituting a new way of life. There are other organisations, such as political parties, churches and various voluntary organisations that have the resources and facilities for helping to develop a culture for autonomy. My appeal, however, like Gorz's, is primarily to trade unionists by virtue of their unique, historical position of being entrusted with the task of improving the lives of the vast majority dependent on the capitalist system.

Why should a culture for autonomy be the foundation of a culture of opposition? Could it not just as easily spawn political quietism?

Most people attempt to carve out spaces for autonomy within the confines of their dependence on the capitalist system. These spaces for autonomy are mostly in the private sphere and thus pose no threat to the capitalist system. But, I have argued, these spaces are, for a growing number of people, insufficiently resourced to enable a meaningful exercise of autonomy. Further, this is very likely to remain the case given the continuing dependence of the vast majority on a capitalist system that is pursuing a course which is increasingly at odds with what most people need. Autonomy has become an urgent need. Capitalism cannot satisfy this need, at least not for a majority. Somehow we have to develop the means of satisfying our need for autonomy ourselves. I have maintained that this involves the development of a culture for autonomy.

In order to develop a culture for autonomy people will need more time and space than they currently have. This cannot be achieved without an emancipatory politics of time. In other words it cannot be achieved without political opposition to the capitalist system.

The purpose of an emancipatory politics of time is the expansion of the sphere of autonomy. This will enable people to be more autonomous. Now, satisfying the need for autonomy is quite a different matter from satisfying our need for food, for example. Whereas there is a limit to the food that we need, this is not so for autonomy. The exercise of autonomy delivers its own satisfactions: it supplies people with a sense of well-being and fulfilment, it is enlivening and, importantly, it *generates the need for more autonomy.* As people become more autonomous they become more resistant to unnecessary restrictions on their autonomy, and seek a further expansion of their sphere of autonomy. Herein resides the oppositional potential of a culture for autonomy.

Bibliographic References and Notes

1 Introduction: Changing Times and the Left

1. For useful, concise and clear analyses, see Ralph Mili-band, *Capitalist Democracy in Britain* (Oxford: Oxford University Press, 1984) and Leo Panitch, 'Capitalism, Socialism and Revolution: The Contemporary Meaning of Revolution in the West' in Ralph Miliband, Leo Panitch and John Saville (eds), *Socialist Register*, 1989 (London: The Merlin Press, 1989) pp. 1–29.
2. For a critical discussion of 'the more peaceful "consumer Communist" route to revolution', as Kate Soper puts it, see Kate Soper, *Troubled Pleasures: Writings on Politics, Gender and Hedonism* (London: Verso, 1990) especially pp. 45–70.
3. The routine attack on one-party states is ironic given that in the liberal democracies of the advanced capitalist socie-ties all major parties are parties of and within capitalism.
4. As for example the Red and Green alliances in Germany. In Britain the most promising development on this front is the socialist movement.
5. For an excellent discussion of the sources of differences among Greens, see Andrew Dobson, *Green Political Thought: An Introduction* (London: Unwin Hyman, 1990).
6. Raymond Williams, 'Mining the Meaning: Key Words in the Miners' Strike', *New Socialist* (March 1985) p. 7.
7. Very useful on detailing the loss of civil liberties is Peter Thornton, *Decade of Decline: Civil Liberties in the Thatcher Years* (London: National Council for Civil Lib-erties, 1989).
8. For a very useful discussion, see Philip Mattera, *Off the Books: The Rise of the Underground Economy* (London: Pluto Press, 1985).
9. Zygmunt Bauman, *Intimations of Postmodernity* (London: Routledge, 1992) p. 49.
10. *Ibid.*, p. 50.
11. *Ibid.*, p. 51.
12. Frank Mort, 'The Politics of Consumption', in Stuart Hall and Martin Jacques (eds), *New Times: The Changing Face of Politics in the 1990s* (London: Lawrence and Wishart, 1989) p. 170).

13. Robert Bocock, *Consumption* (London: Routledge, 1993) p. 106.

14. Anthony Giddens, *New Rules of Sociological Method: A Positive Critique of Interpretive Sociologies* (London: Hutchinson, 1976) p. 114.

15. Anthony Giddens, *Modernity and Self-Identity: Self and Society in the Late Modern Age* (Cambridge: Polity Press, 1991) p. 32.

16. *Ibid.*, p. 81.

17. *Ibid.*, p. 80.

18. See, for example, Floya Anthias and Nira Yuval-Davis, *Racialized Boundaries: Race, Nation, Gender, Colour and Class and the Anti-Racist Struggle* (London: Routledge, 1993) especially pp. 190–8.

19. Giddens, *Modernity and Self-Identity*, p. 214.

20. See Christopher Lasch, *The Culture of Narcissism: American Life in an Age of Diminishing Expectations* (London: Abacus, 1980) and *The Minimal Self: Psychic Survival in Troubled Times* (London: Pan Books, 1985).

21. Rosalind Brunt, 'The Politics of Identity', in Hall and Jacques, *New Times*, p. 150.

22. Jean-François Lyotard, 'An Interview', *Theory, Culture and Society*, vol. 5, nos. 2–3 (1988).

23. Claus Offe, *Contradictions of the Welfare State* (London: Hutchinson, 1984) especially pp. 182–93.

24. Theodor Adorno, *The Culture Industry: Selected Essays on Mass Culture* (London: Routledge, 1991) p. 166.

25. Jürgen Habermas, *Autonomy and Solidarity: Interviews* (London: Verso, 1986) p. 179.

26. Rudolf Bahro, *Building the Green Movement* (London: Heretic books, 1986) p. 211.

27. André Gorz, *Paths To Paradise: On the Liberation from Work* (London: Pluto Press, 1985) p. 75.

28. André Gorz, *Critique of Economic Reason* (London: Verso, 1989) p. 49.

29. Habermas notes that 'the peace demonstrations in the autumn of 1983, immediately prior to the stationing of the missiles, reached dimensions previously unimaginable in the history of the Federal Republic ...' In Habermas, *Interviews*, p. 179.

30. Agnes Heller and Ferenc Fehér, *The Postmodern Political Condition* (Cambridge: Polity Press, 1988) p. 10.

31. Herbert Kitschelt, 'New Social Movements and the Decline of Party Organization', in Russel J. Dalton and Manfred Kuechler (eds), *Challenging the Political Order:*

New Social and Political Movements in Western Democra-cies (Cambridge: Polity Press, 1990) pp. 179–208.

32. Giddens, *Modernity and Self-Identity*, p. 209.

33. Mental Health Foundation, *Mental Illness: The Fundamental Facts* (London: Mental Health Foundation, 1990). See also, National Association for Mental Health, *Mind Information: Mental Health Statistics* (London National Association for Mental Health, 1992) and Josephine Logan, *Counselling and Psychotherapy in Nottingham: A Survey of Supply and Demand* (Nottingham: Nottingham Area Health Authority, 1990).

34. See, for example Paulo Freire, *Cultural Action for Freedom* (Harmondsworth: Penguin Books, 1972) especially pp. 51–83.

35. Jürgen Habermas, 'Introduction', in Habermas (ed), *Observations on 'The Spiritual Situation of the Age': Contemporary German Perspectives* (Cambridge, Massachusetts: Massachusetts Institute of Technology Press, 1984) p. 19.

36. *Ibid.*

37. *Ibid.*, p. 20.

38. Habermas refers to the increase in formal regulation as 'juridification'. He writes:

> The expression 'juridification' (*Verrechtlichung*) refers quite generally to the tendency toward an increase in formal (or positive, written) law that can be observed in modern society. We can distinguish here between the *expansion* of law, that is the legal regulation of new, hitherto informally regulated social matters, from the *increasing density* of law, that is, the specialized breakdown of global statements of the legally relevant facts (*Rechtstatbestande*) into more detailed statements.

In Jürgen Habermas, *The Theory of Communicative Action: The Critique of Functionalist Reason*, vol. 2 (Cambridge: Polity Press, 1987) p. 357.

39. Karl Marx and Frederick Engels, 'The German Ideology: A Critique of the Most Recent German Philosophy as Represented by Feuerbach, B. Bauer, and Stirner', in Loyd D. Easton and Kurt Guddat (eds), *Writings of the Young Marx on Philosophy and Society* (New York: Anchor Books, 1967) pp. 467–8.

2   The Dominant Ideology Thesis

1. Cited in A.P. Simonds, 'On Being Informed', *Theory and Society*, vol. 11 (1982) pp. 587–8.

2. Tom Bottomore, 'Foreword' in Nicholas Abercrombie, Stephen Hill and Bryan S. Turner, *The Dominant Ideology Thesis* (London: Allen and Unwin, 1980) p. ix.

3. Ernest Mandel, *Introduction to Marxism* (London: Pluto Press, 1982) p. 29.

4. Comprehensive and clear treatments of the concept of ideology are available in Terry Eagleton, *Ideology: An Introduction* (London: Verso, 1991); Jorge Larrain, *The Concept of Ideology* (London: Hutchinson, 1979); Larrain, *Marxism and Ideology* (London: Macmillan, 1983), and John B. Thompson, *Ideology and Modern Culture: Critical Social Theory in the Era of Mass Communication* (Cambridge: Polity Press, 1990).

5. Abercrombie, *Dominant Ideology Thesis*, pp. 128–40.

6. Very little has changed over the years. In a debate in the House of Commons in 1807 on a Bill which attempted to provide state-aided schooling for the poor a Tory expressed the following sentiments:

> Giving education to the labouring classes ... [would be] prejudicial to their morals and happiness ... it would render them fractious and refractory ... it would teach them to despise their lot instead of making them good servants in agriculture and other laborious employments to which their rank in society has destined them.

Cited in B. Simon, *Studies in the History of Education, 1780–1870* (London: Lawrence and Wishart, 1960) p. 132.

7. Pierre Bourdieu, 'The School as a Conservative Force: Scholastic and Cultural Inequalities' in Roger Dale, Geoff Esland and Madeleine MacDonald (eds), *Schooling and Capitalism* (London: Routledge and Kegan Paul, 1976) p. 113.

8. There is no doubt that IQ as a measure of intelligence is a myth. Analysis of test items reveals that there is nothing at all about the items which merits the description 'scientific'. Most items are ambiguous, and the recognition of this, which might be taken as a sign of intelligence, is penalised. In relation to this point see Alice Heim, *Intelligence and Personality: Their Assessment and Relationship* (Harmondsworth: Penguin Books, 1970). It is also clear that intelligence tests cannot *measure* the complexities and subtleties involved in the normal application of intelligence in everyday life, let alone in practices of critical reflection. At best intelligence tests reflect one

kind of intelligence – that normally associated with 'low-order mental operations'.

More significantly item analyses of intelligence tests reveal that most tests are permeated with cultural bias. In this regard see Clarence J. Karier, 'Testing for Order and Control in the Corporate Liberal State', in Dale, *Schooling and Capitalism*, pp. 128–141, and Karier, 'Business Values and the Educational State', in Dale, *Schooling and Capitalism*, pp. 21–31. Attempts have been made to devise 'culture-free' intelligence tests, but these are insensitive to the fact that the very idea of 'testing' is more normal to some cultures than others. Most tests, however, are constructed by correlating performance on the new test with performance on an established test. Needless to say this practice is tailor-made for the reproduction of cultural bias. This is particularly disconcerting given that one of the most influential tests in the early days was devised by Lewis M. Terman, a self-proclaimed racist and a prominent member of the Eugenics movement. As a consequence of the cultural bias structured into intelligence tests, Paul Henderson points out that 'the behaviour patterns characteristic of the middle-class life situation came to be defined as "intelligent", and were used as the basis for our assessment, both formal and informal, of intelligence'. In Henderson, 'Class Structure and the Concept of Intelligence', in Dale, *Schooling and Capitalism*, p. 147.

9. Louis Althusser, *Essays on Ideology* (London: Verso, 1984), p. 29.
10. *Ibid.*
11 *Ibid.*, p. 38.
12. *Ibid.*
13. Antonio Gramsci, *Selections from the Prison Notebooks*, Q. Hoare and G. Nowell Smith (eds) (London: Lawrence and Wishart, 1971) p. 268.
14. Althusser, *Essays*, p. 56.
15. *Ibid.*
16. Gramsci, *Prison Notebooks*, p. 12.
17. For a clear presentation and critique of Lacan's theory of the unconscious see David Archard, *Consciousness and the Unconscious* (London: Hutchinson, 1984).
18. See in particular Stuart Hall, *The Road to Renewal: Thatcherism and the Crisis of the Left* (London: Verso, 1988).
19. Abercrombie, *Dominant Ideology Thesis*, p. 153.
20. Thompson, *Ideology and Modern Culture*, p. 88.

21. Both Abercrombie and Thompson have made this observation.

22. This view has come to be associated with an uncritical populism in the field of cultural studies. For a useful discussion see Jim McGuigan, *Cultural Populism* (London: Routledge, 1992) especially pp. 124–9. It is, of course, possible to doubt the centrality of one dominant ideology while appreciating that there are ideologies supporting each and every structure of domination. Such a view is implicit in, for example, Steven Seidman, 'Postmodern Social Theory as Narrative with a Moral Intent', in Steven Seidman and David G. Wagner (eds), *Postmodernism and Social Theory: The Debate over General Theory* (Oxford: Basil Blackwell, 1992) pp. 47–81.

23. The IQ myth is a case in point. It is very doubtful that the capitalist class, for example, have given much thought to the concept of intelligence. Yet this concept has come to be defined and applied in ways that serve the interests of the capitalist system, not least by helping to lower the expectations of life prospects among the working class (see (8), above).

24. The right of all women to be treated as economically independent, and thus the right to claim unemployment benefit, is heavily resisted by the state. The state meets demands for this right by a vigorous defence of family values, while at the same time preventing families from acquiring the resources necessary to reproduce themselves.

25. See Conrad Lodziak, *The Power of Television: A Critical Appraisal* (London: Frances Pinter, 1986) especially pp. 37–64.

26. Thompson, *Ideology and Modern Culture*, p. 90.

27. *Ibid.*

28. *Ibid.*, p. 89.

29. *Ibid.*

30. Michael Mann, 'The Social Cohesion of Liberal Democracy' in Anthony Giddens and David Held (eds), *Classes, Power, and Conflict: Classical and Contemporary Debates* (London: Macmillan, 1982) p. 388.

31. Thus Thompson notes that:
    the ongoing reproduction of the social order is probably more dependent on the fact that individuals are embedded in a variety of different social contexts, that they carry out their lives in routine and regularized ways which are not necessarily animated by overarching values and beliefs ...

In Thompson, *Ideology and Modern Culture*, p. 90.

32. In a survey taken in Britain on a sample representative of the total adult population in 1984, 85 per cent were opposed to reduced spending on health and education; 64 per cent opposed the development of a two-tier health service; 69 per cent supported a 'programme whose first priority is combating unemployment rather than inflation'; 70 per cent were in favour of price controls; and 72 per cent believed the gap between high and low incomes to be too great. From *British Social Attitudes: the 1984 Report*, cited in James Curran, 'Rationale for the Right', *Marxism Today* (February 1985) p. 40.

Following a further five years of the Right's ideological programme, support for social democratic policies increased, and declined for right-wing policies. Only 9 per cent supported a policy of reduced taxes and lower social spending; 19 per cent believed that poverty was due to laziness or lack of willpower, and 23 per cent believed that private health care was good for the National Health Service. In Roger Jowell, Sharon Witherspoon and Lindsay Brook (eds), *British Social Attitudes: the 7th Report* (Aldershot: Gower, 1990).

33. For a detailed analysis of this phenomenon see Hilary Wainwright, 'The Limits of Labourism: 1987 and Beyond', *New Left Review*, vol. 164 (July/August 1987) pp. 34–50.

34. See Mann, 'Social Cohesion' in Giddens and Held, *Classes, Power*, pp. 373–95.

35. See the detailed interview study: Fiona Devine, *Affluent Workers Revisited: Privatism and the Working Class* (Edinburgh: Edinburgh University Press, 1992). For a theoretical interpretation that rejects the dominant ideology thesis see Josephine Logan, 'Privatism, Needs and Social Power: An Exploration of Human Motivation in Contemporary Society', doctoral thesis, University of Nottingham (1993).

36. Dieter Wellershoff, 'Germany – A State of Flux' in Habermas, *Observations*, p. 356.

37. Stuart Hall, 'Basic Instincts off target', *Guardian*, 24 November 1993.

3 The Manipulation of Needs Thesis

1. Cited in André Gorz, *Farewell to the Working Class: An Essay on Post-Industrial Socialism* (London: Pluto Press, 1982) pp. 120–1.

2. Christopher Lasch, *The True and Only Heaven: Progress and Its Critics* (New York: Norton, 1991) p. 518.

3. Cited in Herbert Marcuse, *Counterrevolution and Revolt* (Boston: Beacon Press, 1972) p. 19.

4. See for example E. Dichter, *The Strategy of Desire* (London: Boardman, 1960); Gillian Dyer, *Advertising as Communication* (London: Methuen, 1982); Judith Williamson, *Decoding Advertisements* (London: Marion Boyars, 1978), and Janice Winship, 'Sexuality for Sale' in Stuart Hall, Dorothy Hobson, Andrew Lowe and Paul Willis (eds), *Culture, Media, Language* (London: Hutchinson, 1980) pp. 217–223.

5. Robert Bocock, *Consumption* (London: Routledge, 1993) p. 85.

6. Winship, 'Sexuality', in Hall et al. *Culture*, p. 223.

7. See Sebastiano Timpanaro, *The Freudian Slip: Psychoanalysis and Textual Criticism* (London: New Left Books, 1976).

8. See Henri Ey, *Consciousness: A Phenomenological Study of Being Conscious and Becoming Conscious* (Bloomington: Indiana University Press, 1976).

9. Bauman, *Intimations*, pp. 51–2.

10. *Ibid.*, p. 53.

11. Bocock, *Consumption*, p. 67.

12. *Ibid.*, p. 50.

13. Essentially a minority government stole publicly owned assets, then had the audacity to sell what they had stolen to the people from whom they had stolen them.

14. Reported in H. Sahin and J.P. Robinson, 'Beyond the Realm of Necessity: Television and the Colonization of Leisure', *Media, Culture and Society*, vol. 3 (1980) pp. 85–95.

15. Gorz, *Farewell*, p. 1.

16. For a full discussion of autonomy within work, see Gorz, *Critique*, pp. 73–89.

17. Herbert Marcuse, *Eros and Civilization: A Philosophical Inquiry into Freud* (Boston: Beacon Press, 1966) p. 92.

18. Gorz, *Critique*, p. 119.

19. I have essentially adapted the substance of the thinking of the Frankfurt School here. Very useful in this respect is Max Horkheimer, *Critical Theory: Selected Essays* (New York: Continuum, 1982), especially the essay: 'Authority and the Family' pp. 47–128.

20. Ernest Becker, *The Birth and Death of Meaning: An Inter-disciplinary Perspective on the Problem of Man*

(Harmondsworth: Penguin Books, 1972) p. 83.

21. R.D. Laing, *The Divided Self: An Existential Study in Sanity and Madness* (Harmondsworth; Penguin Books, 1965) p. 42.
22. *Ibid.*, pp. 42–3.
23. Karl Marx and Frederick Engels, *Selected Works* (London: Lawrence and Wishart, 1968) p. 219.
24. Marx wrote that beyond the realm of necessity:

    begins the development of human energy which is an end in itself, the true realm of freedom, which, however, can blossom forth only with this realm of necessity as its basis. The shortening of the working-day is its basic prerequisite.

    In Marx, *Capital, Volume III* (London: Lawrence and Wishart, 1968) p. 820.
25. In Britain between 1977 and 1987, the proportion of income servicing debt increased from about 42% to 81%. Transport and housing were the two most important items of expenditure accounting for this increase. Reported in *Guardian*, 16 November 1988.
26. Gorz, *Strategy For Labour: A Radical Proposal* (Boston: Beacon Press, 1967) p. 88.
27. Offe, *Contradictions*, especially pp. 224–7.
28. Theodor Adorno, *Minima Moralia: Reflections from Damaged Life* (London: Verso, 1978) p. 175.
29. Lasch, *Minimal Self*, pp. 32–3.
30. Marcuse, *Counterrevolution*, pp. 49–50.
31. Lucien Sève, *Man in Marxist Theory and the Psychology of Personality* (Hassocks: Harvester, 1978) p. 321.
32. *Ibid.*
33. Gorz, *Critique*, p. 119.
34. *Ibid.*, p. 100.
35. Adorno, *Minima Moralia*, p. 175.
36. Gorz, *Farewell*, p. 97.
37. Giddens, *Modernity and Self-Identity*, p. 9.

4 Privatism and Autonomy

1. Cited in Sève, *Man in Marxist Theory*, p. 308.
2. Elim Papadakis and Peter Taylor-Gooby, *The Private Provision of Public Welfare: State, Market and Community* (Brighton: Wheatsheaf Books, 1987) p. 15.
3. Logan, 'Privatism'. The concept of 'mobile privatism' was first used by Raymond Williams. See Williams, 'Problems of the Coming Period', *New Left Review*, vol. 140 (July/

August 1983) pp. 7–18.

4. In Britain the decline in trade union membership from just over twelve million to eight million (TUC statistics) throughout the 1980s reflects changes in employment patterns and anti-union legislation.

5. Lasch, *Minimal Self*, p. 16.

6. Anthony Giddens, *The Consequences of Modernity* (Cambridge: Polity Press, 1991) pp. 148–9.

7. Rollo May, *Power and Innocence* (London: Fontana, 1976) p. 21.

8. Giddens, *Modernity and Self-Identity*, p. 191.

9. *Ibid.*, p. 174.

10. Jonathan Rutherford, 'A Place Called Home: Identity and the Cultural Politics of Difference', in Rutherford (ed), *Identity: Community, Culture, Difference* (London: Lawrence and Wishart, 1990) p. 24.

11. George Simmel, 'The Metropolis and Mental Life', in Eric and Mary Josephson (eds), *Man Alone: Alienation in Modern Society* (New York: Laurel, 1962) p. 163.

12. *Ibid.*

13. Dick Hebdige, 'After the Masses', in Hall and Jacques, *New Times*, pp. 90–91.

14. *Ibid.*, p. 91. The 'waning of affect' is part and parcel of Fredric Jameson's depiction of postmodernism. See Jameson, *Postmodernism, or The Cultural Logic of Late Capitalism* (London: Verso, 1991). 'Psychic autism', according to Jean Baudrillard, characterises the contemporary individual, which he depicts as schizoid:

> The schizo is bereft of every scene, open to everything in spite of himself, living in the greatest confusion ... What characterizes him is less the loss of the real ... but ... the absolute proximity, the total instantaneity of things, the feeling of no defence, no retreat. It is the end of interiority and intimacy, the overexposure and transparence of the world which traverses him without obstacle. He can no longer produce the limit of his own being ...

In Baudrillard, 'The Ecstasy of Communication', in H. Foster (ed), *The Anti-Aesthetic: Essays on Postmodern Culture* (Port Townsend: Bay Press, 1983) p. 133.

15. Erik H. Erikson and Huey P. Newton, *In Search of Common Ground* (New York: Laurel, 1973) p. 129.

16. Wolf-Dieter Narr, 'Toward a Society of Conditioned Reflexes', in Habermas, *Observations*, p. 50.

17. Marcuse, *Eros*, p. 57.

18. R.D. Laing, *The Politics of Experience* (New York: Ballantine Books, 1968) p. 68.
19. Adorno, *Minima Moralia*, pp. 95–6.
20. Laing, *Politics of Experience*, p. 73.
21. Max Horkheimer, *Eclipse of Reason* (New York: Continuum, 1974) p. 141.
22. In order to understand the decline in autonomy the Frankfurt School focused their attention on the history of the *bourgeois* family, since it was among the upper classes that the decline of the autonomous personality was most marked. Working class families never enjoyed the sphere of autonomy once available to the bourgeois family. Similarly the Frankfurt School directed their attention to the socialisation of upper class boys – girls of whatever class were always granted a more restricted sphere of autonomy.
23. Marcuse, *Eros*, p. 96.
24. Max Horkheimer, *Critique of Instrumental Reason* (New York: Continuum, 1974) p. 12.
25. *Ibid.*, p. 11.
26. University graduates in areas that promote critical rather than technical intelligence, for example the arts and social sciences rather than pure and applied hard sciences, have higher unemployment rates. Among social science, humanities and arts graduates, unemployment is more likely to befall those achieving a First Class Honours standard than lower achieving graduates. Reported in *Independent*, 6 October 1988. In Britain, at least, employers do not seem to want to employ 'the best minds'. Universities are beginning to respond by installing new forms of management, steeped in incompetence and mediocrity, to enact 'reforms' likely to lower standards.

5　Toward a Culture of Opposition

1. Gorz, *Critique*, p. 114.
2. *Ibid.*, p. 120.
3. *Ibid.*
4. Gorz, *Paths*, p. 51.
5. Gorz, *Farewell*, p. 8.
6. Reported in *Guardian*, 24 November 1993.
7. Gorz, *Critique*, p. 200.
8. *Ibid.*, p. 191.
9. Gorz, *Farewell*, p. 72.
10. Gorz, *Critique*, p. 115.

11. *Ibid.*, p. 239.
12. *Ibid.*, p. 228.
13. *Ibid.*, p. 199.
14. *Ibid.*, p. 208. Proposals for funding the guaranteed income, in the context of a general social policy designed to reduce working time, are presented in Gorz, *Farewell*, pp. 126–44; *Paths*, pp. 40–63 and pp. 103–10; and *Critique*, pp. 199-212. Other proposals are presented and discussed in Philippe Van Parijs (ed), *Arguing for Basic Income: Ethical Foundations for a Radical Reform* (London: Verso, 1992).
15. For example we could choose to fulfil our obligation to work 20,000 hours over our working life by working 1,000 hours per year for 20 years, or 2,000 hours per year for 10 years, or we could work alternate years, or work two months in six, and so on. Parents, for example, could plan their working hours in ways that enabled them both to devote as much time as they needed to care for their children. Single mothers would be able to avoid the dilemmas and hardships they currently experience, and through co-ordinated planning with others could share child-rearing responsibilities.
16. For Freire an authentic revolution is not possible without dialogue. Dialogue involves meaningful communication between equals. Freire insists that 'only dialogue truly communicates'. He claims that 'dialogue imposes itself as the way by which men achieve significance as men. Dialogue is thus an existential necessity'. In Paulo Freire, *Pedagogy of the Oppressed* (New York: Herder and Herder, 1970) p. 77.

    Anti-dialogical communication is viewed by Freire as a form of non-communication. It involves among other things 'manipulation, sloganizing, "depositing", regimentation, and prescription', and as such 'cannot be components of revolutionary praxis, precisely because they are components of the praxis of domination'. In *Pedagogy*, p. 121.
17. R.D. Laing, *Self and Others* (Harmondsworth: Penguin Books, 1969) p. 136.
18. See Logan, 'Privatism', pp. 200–11.
19. Logan, 'Ontological Insecurity in Women', *Reflections*, no. 52 (1985).
20. Carl R. Rogers, 'A Theory of Therapy, Personality, and Interpersonal Relationships, as Developed in the Client-centered Framework', in S. Koch (ed), *Psychology: A*

Study of Science. Study 1. Conceptual and Systematic. Vol. 3: Formulations of the Person and the Social Context (New York: McGraw-Hill, 1959) p. 208.

21. Gorz, *Paths*, p. 103.
22. Gorz, *Critique*, p. 233.
23. *Ibid.*, p. 231.

6 Conclusion: On a Culture of Opposition

1. Patrick Jenkin, cited in Michèle Barrett and Mary McIntosh, *The Anti-social Family* (London: Verso, 1982) p. 12.
2. J. Newsom, 'The Education Women Need', *Observer*, 6 September 1964.
3. Peregrine Worsthorne, 'Too Much Freedom', in Maurice Cowling (ed), *Conservative Essays* (London: Cassell, 1978) p. 141.
4. Stephen Enke and Richard Brown, 'Economic Worth of Preventing Death at Different Ages in Developing Countries', *Journal of Biosocial Science*, vol. 4, no. 3 (July 1972), cited in David Dickson, *Alternative Technology and the Politics of Technical Change* (Glasgow: Fontana, 1974) p. 161.
5. Premature death is the outcome of the normal economic relations between the First World and the Third World.
6. Gorz, *Critique*, p. 225.
7. Kate Soper, *On Human Needs: Open and Closed Theories in a Marxist Perspective* (Brighton: Harvester Press, 1981) p. 184.
8. *Ibid.*
9. Trevor Blackwell and Jeremy Seabrook, *The Politics of Hope: Britain at the End of the Twentieth Century* (London: Faber and Faber, 1988) p. 45.
10. The free school movement sprang up in the 1960s, mainly in California, where it still involves up to 10 per cent of children of school age. The main inspirations of the free school movement are A.S. Neill's Summerhill school, and the writings of Paulo Freire and Ivan Illich. See A.S. Neill, *Summerhill: A Radical Approach to Child Rearing* (New York: Hart, 1960) and Ivan Illich, *Deschooling Society* (New York: Harper and Row, 1970).
11. Gerry Adams, *The Politics of Irish Freedom* (Dingle, Co. Kerry, Ireland: Brandon, 1986) p. 138.
12. Habermas, *Legitimation Crisis* (London: Heinemann, 1976).
13. *Ibid.*, p. 73.
14. *Ibid.*, p. 92.

Index

Abercrombie, Nicholas 27,
34–6, 139, 140, 141
action
as autonomous 57–9
and ideology 40, 44, 115
and needs 69
and resources 55–6
Adams, Gerry 127, 148
Adorno, Theodor 16, 67, 71,
87, 88, 137, 144, 146
advertising 45–7
alienation
from politics 12–19, 44, 105
from self 29, 87–9
from work 99
Althusser, Louis 30–2, 86, 140
Anthias, Floya 137
Archard, David 140
automation 6–7, 99–100
autonomy 7, 22–3, 24, 57–9,
74, 78, 82, 84–5, 85–91
capacity for 85, 88, 90, 91,
92, 124
and capitalism 65–8
of capitalist class 52–5
consumer 22, 60–61, 95
culture for 103–13, 117–18,
123–7
within dependence 59–61
and emancipation 85–91
expansion of 55, 93–5,
98–103, 107, 110–13,
117, 123
and identity 23
autonomy
and ideology of individualism 119–121
manipulation of 55–7, 71
and meaning 61–5, 69

autonomy, *continued*
need for 62, 115, 121–3,
134–5
and oppositional politics
130–1
and privatism 67–8
psychological 74
and reproduction of capitalist
system 52–61, 71
and resources 58–9, 62–5,
69, 71, 85, 115, 116–17
and self 62–5, 85–91, 116,
123–4
and socialisation 85–91
underdevelopment of 71,
85–91, 115
in work 59–60, 67
of working class 55

Bharo, Rudolf 17, 137
Barrett, Michèle 148
Baudrillard, Jean 145
Bauman, Zygmunt 8, 48–9,
50–1, 136, 143
Becker, Ernest 63, 143
Blackwell, Trevor 125, 148
Bocock, Robert 9, 46, 51, 137,
143
Bottomore, Tom 139
Bourdieu, Pierre 29, 139
Brook, Lindsay 142
Brown, Richard 148
Brunt, Rosalind 12, 137

capitalism and postmodernity 3,
5–9, 21–2
capitalist class 1, 8, 25
autonomy 52–5
ideology 26–30, 37–40

Published by Pluto Press

The Human Nature Debate

Social Theory, Social Policy and the Caring Professions

Harry Cowan

The idea of human nature is centuries old. Yet epithets like 'human greed', 'natural inequalities' and 'you can't change the world' still underpin discussion in everyday life as well as in the academic arena. This book challenges such notions and argues that the manifestations of the human nature idea are socially and politically, rather than philosophically, grounded. The book's scope is wide, spanning the social science disciplines and, unlike other texts in the field, incorporates everyday social and political examples into the academic.

Cowan demonstrates how theories of human nature must be related to their intellectual, historical and social roots by analysing biological, psychological and social models, assessing the impacts of Freudianism, behaviourism, existentialism and Marxism upon social theory, policy and caring professions, and evaluating the political significance of racist and sexist accounts.

ISBN hardback: 0 7453 0740 X   softback: 0 7453 0741 8

Order from your local bookseller or contact the publisher on
0181 348 2724.

Pluto Press
345 Archway Road, London N6 5AA
5500 Central Avenue, Boulder, Colorado 80301, USA

Published by Pluto Press

Socialism: What Went Wrong?

An Inquiry into the Theoretical and Historical Sources
of the Socialist Crisis

Irwin Silber

Clearly written, sharply argued and highly stimulating, this book is a profound analysis of the inherent flaws in Marxist-Leninist orthodoxy which undermined, and eventually destroyed, socialism in the Soviet Union.

Silber's critique draws its strength from an historical examination of the critical turning points in communist ideology by means of which he exposes the theoretical and programmatic problems of the Soviet model and the contradictions of the socialist ideal. In the aftermath of the collapse of the Soviet Union, he concludes, we must understand what went wrong, and why, if we hope to build a new socialist movement in the future. Irwin Silber brings to this inquiry the accumulated experience of more than half a century as an activist on the American left.

'*Socialism: What Went Wrong* raises many of the essential questions that we have to consider in constructing a truly democratic left alternative'
Prof. Manning Marable, Columbia University

ISBN hardback: 0 7453 0715 9   softback: 0 7453 0716 7

Order from your local bookseller or contact the publisher on
0181 348 2724.

Pluto Press

345 Archway Road, London N6 5AA
5500 Central Avenue, Boulder, Colorado 80301, USA

Published by Pluto Press

YOUR RIGHTS
The Liberty Guide

Edited by John Wadham

Attacks on civil liberties are on the increase in the United Kingdom. *Your Rights*, compiled by Liberty (the National Council for Civil Liberties), provides an up-to-date comprehensive guide to civil rights and the law (in England and Wales) for the lay reader as well as for those working in the legal and advice professions. Based on Liberty's own advice sheets, the guide explains legal rights, and highlights aspects of the law which adversely affect civil rights.

Each section of the book is written by an expert in the relevant field: the right of peaceful protest; the right of free expression; the right of privacy; the right to know; the right to complain; the rights of suspects; the rights of defendants; the rights of prisoners; the right not to be discriminated against; the rights of immigrants; the rights of mental patients; the rights of children and young people; the rights of workers; the rights of travellers.

ISBN hardback: 0 7453 0778 7   softback: 0 7453 0779 5

Order from your local bookseller or contact the publisher on
0181 348 2724.

Pluto Press
345 Archway Road, London N6 5AA
5500 Central Avenue, Boulder, Colorado 80301, USA